Success in Mini...

# Why
## Non-Tithing Christians Become Poor

## ...and How
## Tithing Christians Can Become Rich

# Dag Heward-Mills

Excerpts in Chapters 11 and 12 from: *The Jewish Phenomenon* by Steven Alan
Silbiger. Copyright © 2000 by Steven Alan Silbiger. Used by permission of Rowman
& Littlefield Publishing Group, Lanham, MD.

Excerpts in Chapter 13 from: *Thou Shall Prosper* by Rabbi Daniel Lapin. Copyright
© 2000 by Rabbi Daniel Lapin. Reproduced with permission of John Wiley & Sons,
Inc., Hoboken, NJ.

Copyright © 2009 Dag Heward-Mills

First published by Lux Verbi.BM (Pty) Ltd. 2010

Published by Parchment House 2011
2nd Printing 2011

ISBN: 978-9988-8505-1-7

Printed by
ChristianBookPrinting.co.uk
Somersham Cambridgeshire UK

E mail Dag Heward-Mills :
evangelist@daghewardmills.org

Find out more at:
www.daghewardmills.org

Write to:
P.O. Box 114
Korle-Bu
Accra
Ghana

# Dedication

To
### Dr. Charles Osei
Thank you for being a personal friend and for your
commitment through the years.

# Contents

# Section 1

# Why Non-Tithing Christians
# Become Poor

*Chapter 1*

# Six Reasons Why Non-Tithers Become Poor

**1.  Non-tithers become poor because they have nothing to harvest.**

FOR THEY HAVE SOWN THE WIND, AND THEY SHALL REAP THE WHIRLWIND: it hath no stalk: the bud shall yield no meal: if so be it yield, the strangers shall swallow it up.

Hosea 8:7

Prosperity in its most basic form consists of someone sowing a seed and later harvesting the returns. Not paying your tithes separates you from this most basic principle of sowing and reaping. When you do not pay your tithes you harm your finances because you take away the foundations of prosperity.

## 2. Non-tithers become poor because they do not attract blessings on their lives.

BRING YE ALL THE TITHES into the storehouse, that there may be meat in mine house, and prove me now herewith, saith the Lord of hosts, if I will not open you the windows of heaven, and POUR YOU OUT A BLESSING, that there shall not be room enough to receive it.

Malachi 3:10

Tithing attracts varied kinds of blessings because that is what the Word of God says. A person who is blessed is favoured and helped. Our lives on earth are very difficult. Jacob said of his life when Pharaoh asked him, "How old art thou?" "And Jacob said unto Pharaoh, The days of the years of my pilgrimage are an hundred and thirty years: FEW AND EVIL HAVE THE DAYS OF THE YEARS OF MY LIFE BEEN, and have not attained unto the days of the years of the life of my fathers in the days of their pilgrimage" (Genesis 47:9).

Job also said that the days of man were few and full of trouble. Even without a specific curse on your life you will encounter many problems and much difficulty. When you do not pay your tithe there is no blessing to counteract the existing problems of this life. How can you do well in life if no word of blessing is spoken over your miserable existence? Do not be surprised at the mounting poverty in your life if you do not pay tithes. The blessing that makes rich and adds no sorrow comes abundantly on the tither.

## 3. Non-tithers become poor because they are cursed.

Will a man rob God? Yet ye have robbed me. But ye say, Wherein have we robbed thee? In tithes and offerings.

YE ARE CURSED WITH A CURSE: for ye have robbed me, even this whole nation.

Malachi 3:8-9

There is a specific curse for people who do not pay tithes. It is one of the top twenty-five curses in this world. This curse on non-tithers only comes to compound the existing multiplicity of curses handed down to us from Adam, Noah and other generations. The curse on people who do not tithe synergistically works with the curses that your parents and ancestors may have incurred on themselves and their descendants. Almost all of us are descendants of people who were cursed for one reason or another through the things that they did.

One day, I became very worried when I discovered that it was likely that my ancestors were slave traders. I found out that there was an ancient fort built right in my father's hometown which must have been used for slave trading. Obviously, I was the descendant of someone who was not sold into captivity. I was therefore likely to be the descendant of someone who sold his brother. Selling your brother would surely bring a curse into your family. Have you ever wondered why places that traded their brothers for trinkets and mirrors are the most poverty-stricken parts of the world today?

Not paying your tithes inflicts a severe additional curse to your life. Don't forget that you are already labouring under Adam's curse. You are also battling with the curse of Ham, if you are a descendant of Ham.

DEAR FRIEND, HOW MUCH MORE CAN YOU TAKE? IS IT NOT TIME TO DO SOMETHING THAT BRINGS A BLESSING? You need the blessing of a tithe payer to counteract all these terrible curses! Is it any wonder that you are becoming poorer as you refuse to pay your tithes?

## 4. Non-tithers become poor because devourers constantly eat their wealth.

AND I WILL REBUKE THE DEVOURER for your sakes, and he shall not destroy the fruits of your ground; neither shall

3

your vine cast her fruit before the time in the field, saith
the Lord of hosts.

Malachi 3:11

The greatest blessing for paying tithes is that God rebukes the
devourer for you. When you listen to government leaders of
poor countries you get the impression that all their problems
would be over if they were to have a little extra money.
Unfortunately, this is not the case. Places which receive a lot of
financial aid typically remain poor. This paradoxical picture
exists because of the inability of the recipients to retain the
money they receive.

Can you imagine what you would need to fill a bucket riddled
with holes? If riches were defined as a bucket full of water, you
would need so much of it to fill such a bucket. But when the
holes are blocked you need just a little water to fill the bucket.

This is the mysterious blessing of the rebuked devourer. After
the devourer is rebuked, it takes just a little to make you a rich
person. When you are without this blessing you will seek better
jobs and earn more money but always fail to become rich. When
the devourer is rebuked, you may not earn that much but your
bucket will fill quickly and soon begin to overflow.

Dear friend, this is what God promises to do when you pay
your tithes. Move away from poverty today and receive the
blessing of the rebuked devourer. Have you ever wondered why
people get bigger and fatter in their middle ages? Often they are
not eating more. In fact, many middle aged people go on diets
to lose weight and still put on weight. What is the reason for the
increase in weight? As people get older, their metabolism slows
down. In other words the fire that burns up the fat slows down.
If the metabolic fire in the body was consuming ten units of fat
every day, it may drop to five units.

Suddenly, you would start to have an increase of an extra five
units of fat available every day. With almost no effort, you put
on weight and become broader and wider. That is why you can
know someone's age by his or her size. As you get older your

metabolism drops, (the devourer is rebuked) and the weight gain (prosperity) occurs.

Indeed, non-tithers become poorer because of the presence of unchecked devourers in their lives.

## 5.    Non-tithers become poor because the fruits of their fields are constantly destroyed.

And I will rebuke the devourer for your sakes, and HE SHALL NOT DESTROY the fruits of your ground; neither shall your vine cast her fruit before the time in the field, saith the Lord of hosts.

Malachi 3:11

The senseless loss of what you have gained through wastage, careless management, neglect, fire, accidents, riots, stealing, and even war are painful but really the works of the destroyer.

One of the great blessings of tithing is to have the destroyer rebuked. The destroyer is the brother to the devourer. The difference between the destroyer and the devourer is that the destroyer removes your wealth in a painful and mindless fashion. It is more painful to see the destroyer at work because there is no sense in the loss that you experience. Begin to pay your tithes and God has promised to rebuke the destroyer.

## 6.    Non-tithers become poor because they lose their fruits before they get a chance to harvest.

And I will rebuke the devourer for your sakes, and he shall not destroy the fruits of your ground; neither shall your vine CAST HER FRUIT BEFORE THE TIME in the field, saith the Lord of hosts.

Malachi 3:11

Another reason why non-tithers become poor is that the fruits of their harvest are lost before they get a chance to harvest them. Non-tithers are cursed with the "failed harvest". A failed harvest is failure to reap the corresponding and appropriate harvest for what you have invested.

Someone confidently taught that if you worked hard you would be rich. He continued, "People who are not rich do not work hard. People in developing countries should just roll up their sleeves and get to the job and prosperity will be their portion."

But if you look around, you will discover many people who work very hard but are not rich! You will find people who work their heads off twelve hours a day and earn almost nothing. Yet a few miles from them you will find people who work for an hour a day and yet earn millions.

Yes, it is true that hard work should lead to prosperity but in many cases it does not. A bus driver in Sweden earns nineteen times what an equally good bus driver in Ghana earns. Why is this? Why don't they reap the same amounts for the same hours of work and the same jobs? Why does one sow a hundred seeds and reap a hundred harvests and another sow a hundred seeds and reap twenty-three harvests?

This is where you find out how real failed harvests are. A failed harvest is the failure of someone to reap the corresponding and appropriate harvest for what he has invested. Many people experience this kind of failed harvest.

Often the causes of a failed harvest are beyond the power of the person experiencing the failed harvest. Why does a Mexican earn so little for his efforts compared to his fellow human being five miles across the border in America? Why is it that the fellow on American soil puts in the same amount of time and effort as a Mexican but earns nineteen times more? The causes and solutions of this dilemma are beyond an individual's ability to correct. But God almighty promises the tither that He will prevent the harvest from falling unceremoniously to the ground. He will not allow your fruits to fall before the harvest time.

Is it any wonder that tithing is a major key to real prosperity? Are you surprised that non-tithers can become poorer by keeping ten percent of their income away from God?

What can you do without the help of God? How far can you go if God does not help you? It is time to begin tithing so that your profits will not be cast to the ground before you can enjoy them.

*Chapter 2*

# The Curses That Follow Non-Tithers

Not paying tithes activates several different curses. Many people think that not tithing only sets in motion the "curse of Malachi". But not tithing sets in motion much more than the curse of Malachi. It sets in motion several other curses which have devastating effects and that is what this chapter is all about.

What is a curse anyway? A curse can be defined in many ways. These twelve definitions of a curse will help you to understand what it means to be under a curse. I cannot imagine what it means to be under multiple curses.

## The Twelve Definitions of a Curse

1.  A cursed person is someone who will experience persistent frustration.

2.  A cursed person is someone who is behind and below in everything.

3.    A cursed person is someone on whom a specific evil has been invoked.

4.    A cursed person is someone who is plagued with mysterious freak incidents.

5.    A cursed person is someone who is a persistent failure.

6.    A cursed person is someone who is persistently rejected and set aside.

7.    A cursed person is someone who is never chosen.

8.    A cursed person is someone who is unable to redirect his life in a positive direction.

9.    A cursed person is someone who is bereft of critically important information.

10.   A cursed person is someone who is constantly assigned to the bad option.

11.   A cursed person is someone who only encounters bad people.

12.   A cursed person is someone who is always last and ends as the loser no matter how he starts.

## EIGHT CURSES THAT FOLLOW NON-TITHERS

**1.    People who do not pay tithes are cursed with the curses of Malachi the prophet.**

**Will a man rob God? Yet ye have robbed me. But ye say, Wherein have we robbed thee? In tithes and offerings. Ye are cursed with a curse: for ye have robbed me, even this whole nation.**
**Malachi 3:8-9**

One of the specific curses in the Bible is Malachi's curse for not tithing. This curse involves the release of the devourer, the destroyer and the failed harvest into your life. The devourer, the destroyer and the failed harvest are discussed in the previous chapter.

## 2.  People who do not pay tithes are cursed with the curse that comes on thieves.

The Bible shows us two interesting curses that relate to people who steal. One is a general curse that God has declared on *thieves in general* and the other is a specific curse for *stealing from God* Himself.

Did you know that there is no need to curse someone who steals from you because there is a general curse on anyone who steals? A thief is already an accursed person! The curse that will follow every thief was declared by the prophet Zechariah.

In this curse, the Lord declares that He will enter the house of the thief and consume everything including the timber and the stones. After this curse comes to pass, the thief will be left with nothing, not even a place to live! The thief may steal millions but this curse will turn the millions into "smoke". The thief will not be able to use the things he has stolen and he will never truly enjoy them. Imagine what this kind of curse would do to a non-tither. He will never benefit from all the tithes he stole from God.

> **Then said he unto me, This is the curse that goeth forth over the face of the whole earth: for every one that stealeth shall be cut off as on this side according to it; and every one that sweareth shall be cut off as on that side according to it.**
>
> **I will bring it forth, saith the LORD of hosts, and it shall enter into the house of the thief, and into the house of him that sweareth falsely by my name: and it shall remain in the midst of his house, and shall consume it with the timber thereof and the stones thereof.**
>
> **Zechariah 5:3-4**

3.    People who do not pay tithes are cursed with the curse that comes on those who dare to steal from God.

**The eyes of the Lord are in every place, beholding the evil and the good.**

**Proverbs 15:3**

It is bad enough to steal but do you really want to steal from God? God has declared in His Word that not tithing is stealing from Him. God sees the non-tither as a thief. All the curses that are due thieves are therefore determined on non-tithers.

But a further debilitating curse is determined on non-tithers for *stealing from God* Himself. "Yet ye have robbed me. But ye say, Wherein have we robbed thee? In tithes and offerings. Ye are cursed with a curse: for ye have robbed me, even this whole nation" (Malachi 3:8-9).

You may get away with throwing your shoes at your dog or even your spouse. But throwing your shoes at the American president could get you into jail! You may steal from a mere man and get away with it. But you will not get away with stealing from God. Stealing from God will get you into big trouble. The eyes of the Lord are everywhere, beholding the good and the evil. He sees every penny you take away from His house. You cannot escape when you steal from God. Stealing from God is *a very bad idea* and I would advise you not to do anything like that. Pay your tithes so that you do not become a doubly accursed thief!

4.    People who do not pay tithes are cursed with the curses that come upon all who break the law.

**Cursed be he that confirmeth not all the words of this law to do them. And all the people shall say, Amen.**

**Deuteronomy 27:26**

The curses on those who break the law are outlined in the

twenty-eighth chapter of Deuteronomy. The curses on people who break the Law therefore affect those who do not pay tithes.

For breaking the Law, there are fifteen curses upon children and material prosperity, thirty curses of sickness, crop failure, war, captivity, business failure and poverty; and twenty-six new and repeated curses of defeat, captivity, sickness, persecution and insanity. You must watch out for this long list of curses when you do not pay tithes (Deuteronomy 28).

**a) Fifteen curses upon children and material prosperity you must watch out for when you do not pay tithes:**

1. You will be cursed in the city (v 16)

2. You will be cursed in the field (v 16 )

3. Your baskets and storehouses will be cursed (v 17)

4. Your children will be cursed (v 18)

5. Your crops will be cursed (v 18)

6. Your herds will not increase (v 18)

7. Your flocks will not increase (v 18)

8. You will be cursed when you come in (v 19)

9. You will be cursed when you go out (v 19)

10. Jehovah will send cursings upon you (v 20)

11. He will send vexation (v 20)

12. He will send rebukes (v 20)

13. You will fail in all you do (v 20)

14. You will be destroyed eventually (v 20)

15. You will quickly perish(v 20)

**b) Thirty more curses of sickness, crop failure, war, captivity; business failure and poverty you must watch out for when you do not pay tithes:**

1. Pestilence cleaving to you (v 21-22)

2.  Death – consumed off the land (v 21-22)

3.  Consumption (v 22; Lev. 26:16)

4.  Fever (v 22; Lev. 26:16)

5.  Inflammation (v 22)

6.  Extreme burning (v 22)

7.  Sword (v 22; Lev. 26:17,25,42)

8.  Blasting (v 22; Lev. 26:19)

9.  Mildew (v 22)

10. Heaven as brass ( v 23; Lev. 26:19)

11. Earth as iron (v 23;Lev. 26:20)

12. Drought, dust - no rain (v 24)

13. Destruction because of long drought (v 24)

14. Smitten before enemies (v 25; Lev. 26:17-39)

15. Going out one way, fleeting seven ways (v 25)

16. Removed into all kingdoms of earth (v 25)

17. Bodies eaten by fowls and beasts ( v 26)

18. No help in driving them off ( v 26)

19. Botch of Egypt (v 27)

20. Emerods (v 27)

21. Scab (v 27)

22. Itch (v 27)

23. No healing (v 27 )

24. Madness (v 28)

25. Blindness (v 28)

26. Astonishment of heart (v 28)

27. Groping at noonday (v 29)

28. No prosperity (v 29)

29. Oppressed and spoiled forever (v 29)

30. No man will save you (v 29)

**c) Twenty-six new and repeated curses of defeat, captivity, sickness, persecution and insanity that you must watch out for when you do not pay tithes**

1. Betroth a wife and an enemy shall capture and ravish her (v 30)

2. Build a house and an enemy shall take it for his own (v 30)

3. Plant a vineyard and an enemy shall take it (v 30)

4. Your stock will be slain and eaten before your eyes (v 31)

5. Your work animals shall be taken (v 31)

6. They shall not be restored to you (v 31)

7. Your sheep will be taken away by enemies (v 31)

8. You will have no man to deliver you (v 31)

9. Your sons and daughters shall be given to other people as slaves (v 32)

10. You will long for deliverance for them which will never come (v 32)

11. You will be powerless to help them (v 32)

12. Enemies will eat your crops (v 33)

13. They shall enjoy the labour of your hands (v 33)

14. You will be oppressed and crushed always (v 33)

15. You will be mad when you see your own helplessness (v 34)

16. You will be smitten with a sore botch (boils and ulcers) that cannot be healed (v 35)

17. You and your king will suffer captivity to a foreign nation (v 36)

18. There you will serve idols (v 36)

19. You will become an astonishment, a proverb, and a byword among all nations (v 37)

20. Your crops will be destroyed by locusts (v 38,43)

21. Your vineyards will be eaten by worms (v 39)

22. You will lose your olive crops (v 40)

23. You will not enjoy your sons and daughters because they will become slaves to foreign nations (v 41)

24. The strangers that are among you will be exalted and you will be humbled (v 43)

25. You will borrow from strangers (v 44)

26. They shall be the head and you shall be the tail (v 44)

Indeed, the breaking of the Law is a frightening prospect. Tithing is therefore important for anyone who does not want to experience these wide-ranging curses. As you can see, not paying tithes brings upon you much more than the curse of Malachi.

**5.     People who do not pay tithes are cursed with the curse that comes on those who repay God's goodness to them with evil.**

How did you come by the health you have? How did you come by the strength that you have? How did you come by the job you have? How did you come by the intelligence and opportunities that you have? What hast thou that thou didst not receive? If you did receive all these things from God how come you do not return to Him and honour Him with the firstfruits of your substance?

Throughout the Bible, curses are spoken over ungrateful people who return evil for good. Perhaps, the most severe and frightening of these is found in the hundred and ninth Psalm. In this Psalm, you discover twenty-seven different curses that follow the ingratitude of those who reward good with evil and love with accusations and suspicion. You learn about the future of those who repay good with evil:

"O God of my praise, do not be silent! For they have opened the wicked and deceitful mouth against me; They have spoken against me with a lying tongue. They have also surrounded me with words of hatred, And fought against me without cause. In return for my love they act as my accusers; But I am in prayer. Thus they have repaid me evil for good and hatred for my love.

Appoint a wicked man over him, And let an accuser stand at his right hand. When he is judged, let him come forth guilty, and let his prayer become sin.

Let his days be few; Let another take his office. Let his children be fatherless And his wife a widow. Let his children wander about and beg; And let them seek sustenance far from their ruined homes. Let the creditor seize all that he has, And let strangers plunder the product of his labor. Let there be none to extend lovingkindness to him, nor any to be gracious to his fatherless children. Let his posterity be cut off; in a following generation let their name be blotted out" (Psalm 109:1-13, NASB).

But why would such things apply to someone who does not pay tithes? The answer is simple. God has been good to you. He has blessed you and provided for you. The tithe is an act of worship, an act of remembrance and an act of thanksgiving! Failing to give your tithes is the same as not saying "thank you". Failing to pay your tithes is the same as not remembering and not worshipping God! Not tithing is a manifestation of nonchalance and ingratitude! If you do not tithe, you fall into the category of ungrateful people. You must therefore expect all the twenty-seven curses of Psalm 109 to be your portion from now on. Read the following twenty-seven curses that apply to people who are ungrateful and repay evil for good. They equally apply to people who do not pay tithes nor say "thank you" to God for His blessing.

16

## Twenty-Seven Curses on Ungrateful People

1.  Set a wicked man over him (v 6)

2.  Let Satan stand at his right hand (v 6)

3.  Let him be condemned ( v 7)

4.  Let his prayer become sin (v 7)

5.  Let his days be few ( v 8)

6.  Let another take his office ( v 8)

7.  Let his children be fatherless (v 9)

8.  Let his wife be a widow (v 9)

9.  Let his children be vagabonds continually (v 10)

10. Let his children beg (v 10)

11. Let them seek their breads in desolate places (v 10)

12. Let the extortioner catch all that he has (v 11)

13. Let strangers spoil his labour (v 11)

14. Let none extend him mercy (v 12)

15. Let none favour his children (v 12 )

16. Let his posterity be cut off (v 13)

17. Let their name be blotted out (v 13)

18. Let iniquity of his fathers be remembered with the Lord (v 14)

19. Let not the sin of his mother be blotted out (v 14)

20. Let them be before the Lord continually (v 15)

21. Let the memory of them be cut off from the earth (v 15)

22. Let cursing come to him ( v 17)

23. Let blessing be far from him ( v 17)

24. Let cursing come unto him like water (v 18)

25. Let curses enter him like oil into his bones (v 18)

26. Let curses cling to him like a garment (v 19)

27. Let curses cling to him like a girdle (v 19).

## 6. People who do not pay tithes are cursed with the curse of closed heavens. The heavens over them are become brass.

**And thy heaven that is over thy head shall be brass, and the earth that is under thee shall be iron.**

**Deuteronomy 28:23**

A very significant curse that follows non-tithers is that of a "closed heaven".

"Bring ye all the tithes into the storehouse, that there may be meat in mine house, and prove me now herewith, saith the Lord of hosts, if I will not open you the windows of heaven, and pour you out a blessing, that there shall not be room enough to receive it" (Malachi 3:10).

A specific difficulty that comes upon non-tithers is that the heavens above them are turned into brass. The heavens are usually made of the wind, the clouds and welcoming showers of blessings. Unfortunately, there are no such blessings coming out of a heaven made of brass. The sister curse to the "brass heavens" is that the earth will be made out of iron. "And thy heaven that is over thy head shall be brass, and the earth that is under thee shall be iron" (Deuteronomy 28:23).

Things are difficult as they are anyway. The earth is already cursed because of the sin of Adam. A heaven of brass and an earth of iron will only combine to make sowing and reaping even more difficult. The seeds cannot enter the iron ground below and there will be no rain from the brass heaven above. The curse of the brass heavens and the iron earth is therefore the curse of having an acute shut down of all business and money-earning activities in your life.

Dear friend, why would you want to bring upon yourself such difficulties? It is time to pay tithes and honour the Lord with your substance. Do you want God to take away your ability to earn money? Certainly not!

## 7.    People who do not pay tithes are cursed with the curse of those who forget God.

**The wicked shall be turned into hell, and all THE NATIONS THAT FORGET GOD.**

**Psalm 9:17**

**A voice was heard upon the high places, weeping and supplications of the children of Israel: for they have perverted their way, and THEY HAVE FORGOTTEN THE LORD THEIR GOD.**

**Jeremiah 3:19-21**

There is a curse on all who forget God. According to Jeremiah, you must expect weeping and supplication because you have forgotten the Lord your God. When you do not pay tithes, you demonstrate that you have forgotten that it is God who has given you all that you have. This forgetfulness may be very costly. When you do not pay tithes at the end of every month, you demonstrate on a monthly basis that you do not remember or acknowledge God in your life.

Recently, there was a presidential election in one of the richest nations in the world. The presidential candidate was an outsider and from a minority group in that nation. It was a historic victory which stirred up emotions around the world. I watched with keen interest as the impossible became possible. However, I was greatly disappointed when this new "underdog president" gave his victory speech and did not acknowledge God. I was expecting him to thank God for helping him to achieve his election victory. Instead, he thanked his campaign manager, his wife, his vice-president, the team that worked with him, and even his little children. He even remembered to mention to his children that he would reward them with a new pet.

At the beginning of the speech, I thought that he had forgotten to mention God because of the euphoria of the moment. I thought he would thank God at the end of his speech but I was wrong! The "thank you" to God never came! He never thanked God or even acknowledged that God had played any role in him becoming the president.

I thought it would be even more obvious that he needed to thank God since his victory was won against the odds. His wife seemed to know that they were an unlikely couple to become President and First Lady. In a speech at a post-election event she said, "There is nothing in my background that should make me stand before you at this time."

I honestly thought this president's failure to thank God was a very bad sign and perhaps even a bad omen. Notice what Isaiah said, "I, even I, am he that comforteth you: who art thou, that thou shouldest be afraid of a man that shall die, and of the son of man which shall be made as grass; and FORGETTEST THE LORD THY MAKER, that hath stretched forth the heavens, and laid the foundations of the earth..." (Isaiah 51:12-13).

Dear friend, it is time to remember the God-factor in everything you do. It is time to pay your tithes and say, "I remember God. Every time you pay tithes you say, "All that I am and all that I have comes from God."

**8.    People who do not pay tithes are cursed with the curse that comes upon idol worshippers who would put money before their service to God.**

**Cursed be the man that maketh any graven or molten image, an abomination unto the Lord, the work of the hands of the craftsman, and putteth it in a secret place. And all the people shall answer and say, Amen.**

**Deuteronomy 27:15**

Worshipping idols is the number one sin that brought the wrath of God on the children of Israel. All through the Bible, we are warned against worshipping idols.

## The Rat god

What if I pointed to one of my associate pastors and said, "This is you: Rev. Jack Toronto. I am writing your name under the rat in this picture and I will put it in my office. Anyone who comes into my office will see this ugly rat and ask, "Who is this rat? Why do you call this rat Rev. Jack Toronto? Is Rev. Jack Toronto not one of the senior pastors in this church? Is Rev. Jack Toronto a rat?"

Do you think Rev. Jack Toronto will be happy with that picture? I do not think so. That picture would be an insult because Rev. Jack Toronto is not a rat. He is far greater than a rat. He is far more intelligent than a rat. He is far more handsome than a rat.

God is far greater than a piece of wood or stone. God is far greater than a snake, an eagle or an antelope. Yet, men make images of these creatures and call them God. How could you make an image of an animal and call it God? You can imagine why the wrath of God comes upon idol worshipers.

People who do not pay tithes are equally guilty of worshiping idols. They have made money their god. They obey money! They sacrifice their lives for it! They get up early in the morning for it! They travel long distances for it! They even kill other human beings for it! They have sex with anybody for it! In fact, the modern "money idol" has a stronger control on people than traditional idols of eagles, crabs or lions.

The exhortation from the apostle John was not out of context. "Little children, keep yourselves from idols. Amen" (1 John 5:21). Paying tithes is one of the best ways to keep yourself from idols. The one you pay ten percent of your income to is your God!

*Chapter 3*

# What It Means to Rob God

**Will a man rob God?**

**Yet ye have robbed me.**

**But ye say, Wherein have we robbed thee?**

**In tithes and offerings.**

**Malachi 3:8**

The most famous Scripture on tithing is found in Malachi and it tells us that a man who does not pay tithes steals from God. But does this Scripture really mean what it says? Can a man really steal from God? Would God really allow anyone to steal from Him? Would they not be struck down instantly?

I remember working with people who stole from me. I did not react immediately nor cut them off. Sometimes thieves are given a grace period and allowed to reform. It is all part of the mercies of God. It is this mercy which Christendom has taken for granted.

Indeed, a man can steal from God! And men do steal from God. It is time to repent and turn away altogether from the practice of stealing from God.

## 1. Ten percent of your income is the property of the Lord.

**And all the tithe of the land, whether of the seed of the land, or of the fruit of the tree, is the LORD'S: it is holy unto the LORD.**

**Leviticus 27:30**

The tithe belongs to the Lord! Withholding your tithe is stealing from God. Leviticus 27:30 is a very important Scripture because it reveals that the tithe is actually the Lord's property. Bringing the tithe to the house of God is not the same as giving a gift of something you own.

It is important to have a proper understanding of the tithe. When you think of something as belonging to another, you are less likely to want to keep it illegally. Since the tithe is *not* for you, presenting it to the Lord is *not* the same as "giving". After you have paid your tithe and do not possess any property of the Lord, only then can you say you are giving something to the Lord. Remember this statement, "giving begins *after* you have paid your tithe."

What if an armed robber robbed you in the night and came the next day to present you with gifts for your birthday? He only presents you with something he stole from you! That is what it is like when you do not pay your tithes but present other offerings to the Lord.

## 2. Not paying your tithe is stealing God's property.

**Will a man rob God? Yet ye have robbed me. But ye say, Wherein have we robbed thee? In tithes and offerings.**

**Malachi 3:8**

God says you can steal from Him and you had better believe it!

Many people do not believe that a man can steal from God. A man *can* steal from God but it is dangerous to do so.

If you steal from a poor man you will probably get away with it. But if you steal from an important person, you will get into big trouble. The greater the person, the more dangerous it is to steal from him. Stealing from God is very risky business indeed because, God sees everything and knows each time you steal from Him.

Throwing your shoes at your dog will not get you into trouble. Throwing your shoes at your servant will not get you into much trouble. However, throwing your shoes at the president can get you into serious trouble. The gentleman who threw shoes at President Bush got himself into big trouble and ended up in prison. I am sure he had thrown shoes at other people before but never got into trouble!

Perhaps you have stolen from mere human beings and gotten away with it. But you will not get away with stealing from God.

3.    **The Bible admonishes thieves not to steal anymore.**

**Let him that stole steal no more: but rather let him labour, working with his hands the thing which is good, that he may have to give to him that needeth.**

**Ephesians 4:28**

Many unbelievers are thieves in one way or another. An unbeliever steals at every chance he gets. If it were not for fear of the police or prison there would be much more open stealing. God does not want you to continue the practice of stealing that you learnt in the world.

Christ has redeemed a large group of liars and thieves to Himself and He urges them to leave their old ways behind. The nature of the thief is the nature of the devil. The thief comes to

24

steal to kill and to destroy and we all know who this famous thief is. Why would you want to pattern your life after that of a thief? Now that you are born again do not continue to steal by withholding your tithes. Indeed, God has declared that not paying tithes is stealing from Him.

## 4.    There will be no thieves in Heaven.

**But lay up for yourselves treasures in heaven, where neither moth nor rust doth corrupt, and where thieves do not break through nor steal:**

**Matthew 6:20**

There will be no thieves in Heaven! When you do not pay tithes, you make yourself a thief and therefore unsuitable for Heaven. Could it be that your failure to pay tithes could actually keep you out of Heaven? What if tithing is a more important subject than we have believed? What if these Scriptures are applied literally and you are prevented from entering Heaven because you did not pay tithes?

## 5.    Stealing the tithe destroys your relationship with God.

**Listen to the word of the Lord, O sons of Israel,**

**For THE LORD HAS A CASE AGAINST THE INHABITANTS OF THE LAND,**

**BECAUSE THERE IS no faithfulness or kindness**

**Or knowledge of God in the land.**

**There is swearing, deception, murder, STEALING and adultery.**

**Hosea 4:1-2 (NASB)**

Stealing always destroys relationships. God has a case against thieves. Society has a case against thieves. Stealing destroys your relationship with the society. That is why thieves are put away in prison. Thieves are put in prison because they are anti-social and it is not safe to have them living freely in our midst. A thief destroys his relationship with the person he steals from. When you steal from God it will destroy your relationship with Him.

If one of your servants steals from you, his relationship with you will be destroyed forever. No one trusts a thief. No one feels free with thieves in his house. When you do not pay tithes, you become a thief and this destroys your relationship with your God.

## 6.    Stealing the tithe will cause your demotion.

**For they know not to do right, saith the Lord, who store up violence and ROBBERY in their palaces.**

**Therefore thus saith the Lord God; An adversary there shall be even round about the land; and HE SHALL BRING DOWN THY STRENGTH FROM THEE, and thy palaces shall be spoiled.**

**Amos 3:10-11**

The Scripture above shows how the anger of the Lord is released against thieves. Their strength is brought down and their homes (palaces) are destroyed. Thieves are not promoted. Thieves are not given positions of responsibility. No one gives a thief a sensitive position. You would not trust a known thief with your purse. Why do you think God would trust you with His money? God may have wanted to pass large amounts of money through your hand but He will not be able to do that because you are known to regularly steal His money.

## 7.    Withholding the tithe robs the church of its ability to function properly.

Robbing the church of the tithe robs the church of the ability to build the necessary facilities. Stealing the tithe robs the church of the ability to employ good people to work for the Lord. Stealing the tithe is therefore a very serious crime.

I once heard someone advocate the death sentence for people who stole money from the state. His argument was simple. Someone who robs a nation of large amounts of money actually deprives the country of the roads it could have built. The lack of good roads causes many accidents and takes many lives. This fellow argued that the man who had caused financial loss to the state had indirectly murdered many people through road accidents. He also contended that money stolen from the state prevented the government from building necessary hospitals that would save lives. This, he also argued, was an indirect way in which the thief committed murder. Because of these he declared that the death penalty should be applied to people who stole large amounts of money from the state.

This line of thought can be applied to people who withhold the tithe and rob God's house of its rightful income. In so doing, they prevent the church from doing all the things that it could have done. Souls are lost and perish in Hell because people do not pay their tithes. Do not rob the church of the ability to hold crusades and win souls.

## 8. Stealing brings the wrath of God upon you.

**The people of the land have used oppression, and EXERCISED ROBBERY, and have vexed the poor and needy: yea, they have oppressed the stranger wrongfully.**

**And I sought for a man among them, that should make up the hedge, and stand in the gap before me for the land, that I should not destroy it: but I found none.**

**THEREFORE HAVE I POURED OUT MINE INDIGNATION UPON THEM; I have consumed them with the fire of my wrath: their own way have I recompensed upon their heads, saith the Lord GOD.**

**Ezekiel 22:29-31**

27

Often, when a thief is discovered, the wrath and contempt of society are poured out on him. Police are called in and the person is arrested.

In primitive societies, instant justice is meted out and the thief could be beaten to death.

In some societies the thief's hand is cut off so that he will not steal anymore. All these are expressions of wrath towards thieves.

Is it any wonder that God's anger is stirred up against those who steal from Him? Do you expect God to behave any differently towards people who steal from Him? Indeed, God is angry with all thieves who have deprived His house of what belongs to Him. When you do not pay tithes, do not expect the blessing of God. Expect the wrath of God to come upon you!

*Chapter 4*

# Twenty Spiritual Problems of People Who Do Not Pay Tithes

Most people who do not pay tithes are in a poor spiritual state. You will notice that each one of the reasons in this chapter is related to the spiritual well-being of the person. Notice also how stopping of the tithe is often a first sign of spiritual decline.

**1.    People do not pay tithes because they are disloyal.**

**Then saith one of his disciples, Judas Iscariot, Simon's son, which should betray him, Why was not this ointment sold for three hundred pence, and given to the poor?**

**John 12:4-5**

One of the reasons why people do not pay tithes is because they are disloyal to God, to their church and to their pastor. Loyalty to a vision is revealed by the amount of money that people contribute to it. This is why political parties constantly assess the support they get for their campaigns. They want to know who gave what. They want to know how much support they are getting from certain quarters. The amount of support they receive defines the loyalties of their different supporters. The amount of money donated to the party is seen as an indication of the support and the loyalty of the contributor.

The tithes that people pay will always give you a good picture of how loyal they are to the vision of the church.

## 2.    People do not pay tithes because they are rebellious.

**But the people took of the spoil, sheep and oxen, the chief of the things which should have been utterly destroyed, to sacrifice unto the Lord thy God in Gilgal. And Samuel said, Hath the Lord as great delight in burnt offerings and sacrifices, as in obeying the voice of the Lord? Behold, to obey is better than sacrifice, and to hearken than the fat of rams. For rebellion is as the sin of witchcraft, and stubbornness is as iniquity and idolatry. Because thou hast rejected the word of the Lord, he hath also rejected thee from being king.**

**1 Samuel 15:21-23**

A rebellious person will not pay tithes. Like Saul, he will not obey the voice of the Lord. He may pretend to sacrifice other things for the Lord. But he rebels against the commandment of the Lord to give ten percent of his income to God. Many rebellious people have an outward show of obedience but in reality, they are very rebellious to God.

Saul is the best example of a rebellious person who presented many sacrifices to the Lord. In spite of his sacrifice to the Lord, the prophet of the Lord saw through the facade and rebuked Saul for disobedience and rebellion.

## 3.     People do not pay tithes because they only obey sections of the Word of God.

**Therefore, as ye abound in every thing, in faith, and utterance, and knowledge, and in all diligence, and in your love to us, see that ye abound in this grace also.**

**2 Corinthians 8:7**

Most Christians obey sections of the Word of God. One day, I met a brother who had been married for a few years. He was distraught because his wife, who was seen as an ideal Christian in the church was not obeying him.

In his exasperation, he asked another brother who was getting married in a few weeks, "Are you going to go through six months of marriage counselling which will not be obeyed." This brother was so unhappy because his wife was not fully compliant with the marriage counselling they had received for six whole months.

I smiled to myself and said within me, "Brother, welcome to discovery channel. You have just discovered for yourself that most people only obey sections of the Word of God."

## 4.     People do not pay tithes because they are greedy.

**We shall find all precious substance, we shall fill our houses with spoil:...**

**So are the ways of every one that is greedy of gain; which taketh away the life of the owners thereof.**

**Proverbs 1:13, 19**

Many people are also greedy. Greed is an excessive desire to acquire and possess more than you need, especially with regards to material wealth. Because people want more and more, it does not make sense for them to give away a portion of what they have. It makes more sense to the greedy person to keep as much as he can! Greed is one of the terrible spiritual vices a person can have. Greed destroys lives. Through greed, the church of God is deprived of the tithe. Greed takes away the blessing and opens the door to a curse.

## The Greedy Man and the Envious Man

The story is told of a greedy man and an envious man who lived in the same town. One day, the king called both of them to his palace and told them that he had decided to bless them.

He said to them, "I feel touched and I want to give you something special. Ask me whatever you want and I will do it for you with one condition. Whatever I do for one, I will do twice as much for the other. So the king asked them to think about it.

The greedy man and the envious man immediately began to argue amongst themselves as to who should make his request first. The greedy man did not want to ask first because he wanted to have more than the envious man. The envious man did not want to ask first either because he would be jealous if the greedy man had more than he did.

The two of them argued till the greedy man prevailed upon the envious man to make his request first. The greedy man was happy because he knew he would get twice as much as the envious man. So the king readied himself for the request, knowing he would have to do twice as much for the greedy man.

The whole court stood still as the envious man made his request. He said, "I want you to pluck out one of my eyes."

The greedy man dropped his jaw in unbelief. Everyone was aghast because they knew what it meant. If the envious man had one of his eyes pulled out, the greedy man would have both of his eyes plucked out.

What a sad and painful end to what could have been prosperity and blessings for both the greedy man and the envious man. Instead of becoming rich they became blind. Such is the curse of greed. It robs us of blessings and leads us to the curse.

5. **People do not pay tithes because they are not spiritually minded.**

**For to be carnally minded is death; but to be spiritually minded is life and peace.**

**Romans 8:6**

Only spiritually-minded people can do something like paying tithes. Because most human beings are genuinely in need, it often does not make sense for them to give away any money at all. Indeed, you must be spiritual if you are going to give away some of your money.

Unless a person becomes spiritual enough to override his natural, greedy, selfish and needy state, he cannot come to terms with the fact that he has to pay tithes. This is why men who are carnal do not pay tithes. Unless a person is spiritual enough to override his logical thinking he cannot pay tithes.

6. **People do not pay tithes because they are immature.**

The Bible has two types of teachings: teachings of "milk" and teachings of "meat". The instruction to pay tithes is a teaching of "meat". You cannot expect babies to obey the instructions to pay tithes; strong meat is for the mature.

**For when for the time ye ought to be teachers, ye have need that one teach you again which be the first principles of the oracles of God; and are become such as have need of milk, and not of strong meat... But strong meat belongeth to them that are of full age, even those who by reason of use have their senses exercised to discern both good and evil.**

**Hebrews 5:12, 14**

Once again, it takes great maturity to rise above the carnal reality of our personal lives. Years will go by, and a certain maturing and mellowing of your nature will cause you to recognize the need to give.

When I was younger, I often wondered why western countries gave money to poorer nations. But as I matured, I realised there were many reasons why a rich nation would give money to a poor country. Although many of these are selfish reasons for giving, it still takes maturity to see the need to give.

Indeed, giving is only possible when you have the mind and heart of a mature person. It takes maturity to see beyond the complex maze of the "apparent disadvantages" of giving and to recognize the benefits of giving.

Most countries and individuals who constantly receive aid rarely rise up and prosper. In fact, receiving gifts and donations have been known to kill business initiatives, agricultural initiatives and industry.

But how could a simpleton ever understand any of these things? That is why it takes maturity to even think of giving away money or even paying tithes.

## 7. People do not pay tithes because they do not really believe the Bible.

**Wherefore (as the Holy Ghost saith, to day if ye will hear his voice, Harden not your hearts, as in the provocation, in the day of temptation in the wilderness:**

**Hebrews 3:7-8**

**Take heed, brethren, lest there be in any of you an evil heart of unbelief, in departing from the living God.**

**Hebrews 3:12**

The Bible is the most published and most translated book on earth. It is also the number one bestselling book on earth. Unfortunately, I cannot say that it is obeyed and believed as much as it is bought and sold.

A casual observation of the lives of people will reveal to you that they do not really believe in Heaven or Hell. Even children can tell that some priests and pastors do not believe what they are talking about.

I remember the story of a criminal who was being put to death for his crimes. His cold, stony face revealed no emotion as he was led to the gallows. Just before his execution, the priest began to sing a canticle. The priest's song was about the valley of the shadow of death and about Heaven and Hell.

But the priest had the shock of his life when the hardened criminal asked him to shut up.

"Will you please shut up," said the criminal to the priest. "You don't believe all the things you are saying, do you?"

The priest was taken aback. He was not used to such responses from people who were just about to die. He thought the criminal would pray and cry for mercy.

Sensing the priest's confusion, the criminal said to him, "Listen to me: if I believed the things you said you believed; if the whole of England and Wales were covered with broken bottles, I would crawl over on my hands and knees to tell the last sinner about it."

Indeed, the priest was duly rebuked for not being convincing. If Christians believed in the blessings and curses that are associated with the concept of tithing, every church would have a hundred percent tithe paying congregation.

Unfortunately, most Christians do not really believe the bible. In fact they do not want the bible to be literally true. This is why most churches have a very low percentage of people who pay tithes. There are a lot of people who believe that there is a God. There are a lot of people who have churches and pastors but do not believe the things in the Bible. This is one of the reasons why so few people actually pay tithes!

## 8.　People do not pay tithes because they are backslidden.

**No servant can serve two masters: for either he will hate**

**the one, and love the other; or else he will hold to the one, and despise the other. Ye cannot serve God and mammon.**

**Luke 16:13**

One of the first signs of backsliding is not paying tithes. You must be spiritual and mature to pay tithes. When a person's spiritual life is declining, paying tithes is one of the first things he stops doing.

I remember a discussion I had about the spiritual life of one of my church members. I suspected that he was backsliding but I had no proof. So I called his wife and asked her, "Is your husband okay?"

"Yes," she answered. "He is doing well."

I continued, "Is he backsliding?"

"Of course not," She replied.

Then I asked, "Does your husband pay tithes?"

She answered, "No he does not. He stopped paying some time ago."

I immediately suspected that her husband was indeed backslidden. After several months it was all confirmed that he was indeed backsliding.

Later on, his wife agreed with me that he *began to backslide* at the same time as when he stopped paying his tithes.

Backsliders do not pay tithes! Perhaps the reason you do not pay tithes is that you are backsliding.

9.     **People do not pay tithes because they have very little love for God.**

**Moreover, BECAUSE I HAVE SET MY AFFECTION TO THE HOUSE OF MY GOD, I have of mine own proper good, of gold and silver, which I have given to the house of**

**my God, over and above all that I have prepared for the holy house,**

**1 Chronicles 29:3**

Love is such a beautiful thing. If you loved God, there would be nothing too difficult for you to do. David loved the Lord and he set his affection on the house of God. Because of this, he bestowed much gold and silver on the house of God. He prepared many gifts and gave them to the house of God.

Being "in love" with someone is euphoric, to say the least. When you are in love with someone, you are emotionally obsessed with the person. You go to bed thinking of the person. When you rise, that person is the first thought on your mind. You long to be together. Spending time together is like being in Heaven.

When you hold hands, it seems as if your blood flows together. You could kiss forever if you did not have to go to work. When people are in love embracing stirs up feelings of rapture.

These feelings will make you do anything for the person you love. If you really loved God, you would do anything for Him. When you love someone, you think you are going to make each other very happy. You think that other couples may argue and fight, but your case will be different. Indeed, you are in "love".

When you love someone, you are certain that you will discuss your differences openly. You know that you will always be willing to make concessions for the one you love and you will always reach an agreement. It is hard to believe anything else when you are in love.

Is this the kind of love you offer to God? Do you make concessions for God? Do you agree with Him when He asks you for a tithe?

We have even been led to believe that if we are really in love, it will last forever. We will always have the wonderful feelings that we have at the present moment. Nothing could ever come between us. Nothing will ever overcome our love for each other. We are enamoured and caught up in the beauty and charm of each other's personality. Love is the most wonderful thing we have ever experienced.

Interestingly, we also claim to love God. How come we cannot make concessions for His work? It is because we do not really love God that we are unable to give up anything for Him. Not even the tithe?

Not tithing is the same as not loving God!

Do not say that you love God when you are not prepared to give even ten percent of your increase to Him.

## 10.   People do not pay tithes because they are ignorant.

**And now, brethren, I wot that through ignorance ye did it, as did also your rulers.**

**Acts 3:17**

**And the times of this ignorance God winked at; but now commandeth all men every where to repent:**

**Acts 17:30**

Sometimes, people do not pay tithes because they are ignorant of the Word. That is why I am writing this book. When you go through the Scriptures in this treatise, you will not have an excuse to not pay tithes. The more of the Scripture that I see on the concept of tithing, the more I want to pay my tithes. After reading this line, ignorance will no longer be an excuse for you. The evidence of Scripture is overwhelming. You have no choice but to yield to the Word of God. You can no longer claim ignorance on the doctrine of tithing.

## 11. People do not pay tithes because they are afraid.

**And I was afraid, and went and hid thy talent in the earth: lo, there thou hast that is thine.**

**Matthew 25:25**

Many people do not pay tithes because they are afraid of poverty. They fear: "Will I be able to go through the month. Will I survive if I pay my tithes? This is a common fear, but you must remember that fear is an evil spirit.

If you follow fear, you are following a demon. God has not given us the spirit of fear. Can you imagine where a demon will lead you? If you love God, you must cast out your fears and decide to obey Him.

A quick analysis will reveal that people do things even though they have deep fears within. People get married in spite of their many fears. There are many things that could go wrong in a marriage! There could be unfaithfulness! There could be divorce! There could childlessness! There could be tragedy! There could be poverty!

There could be death! In spite of these fears, people continue to marry and do what they really want to do. Why are you unable to overcome your fears and pay your tithes? It is time to walk by faith and pay tithes. A person who does not pay tithes is living by the spirit of fear.

## 12. People do not pay tithes because they are offended by something the pastor has done and want to punish the pastor by not paying tithes.

There are people who think they are punishing the man of God by not paying tithes. "I will show you where power lies," they say within themselves. "This is the last time I am paying my tithes."

All these are said when they are angry with the pastor. How silly! When you do not pay tithes, you rob God and not the pastor. Have you ever heard the Scripture which says, "Will a man ROB THE PASTOR? Yet ye have robbed me. But ye say, Wherein have we robbed thee? In tithes and offerings."

No Sir! The Bible teaches us that not tithing is *robbing* God and not robbing the pastor. "Will a man rob God? Yet ye have robbed me. But ye say, Wherein have we robbed thee? In tithes and offerings" (Malachi 3:8 ).

No pastor can reward you for paying your tithes. The blessings for tithe paying do not come from the pastor. They come from the Lord. Tithe paying is your obedience to God. It is not your obedience to man! Do not deceive yourself that you are punishing anybody. If you are punishing anyone you are punishing yourself.

## 13. People do not pay tithes because they do not care whether the church exists or not.

**Ye looked for much, and, lo, it came to little; and when ye brought it home, I did blow upon it. Why? saith the LORD of hosts. Because of mine house that is waste, and ye run every man unto his own house. Therefore the heaven over you is stayed from dew, and the earth is stayed from her fruit.**

**Haggai 1:9-10**

Paying your tithes demonstrates your care for the house of God. The tithes are used to maintain the house of the Lord. When you do not pay tithes, the church cannot be built and the work of God cannot go on.

Many Christians do not really care whether the church exists or not. They say to themselves, "I can always go to another church." They assume the church will always be there. They have a nonchalant attitude towards the existence of the church. This attitude attracts a curse.

40

This indifferent attitude is characteristic of the man who does not know the value of the house of God. David said, "One thing have I desired that I will dwell in the house of the Lord forever." King David wanted to be in the house of God.

People who love the house of God love to pay tithes. It is their joy to see God's house being built. After all, the house of God is where they would love to dwell forever. It is their joy to see that the house of God is more beautiful than their own house. When you love God, you will spend more money on the house of God than on your own house.

## 14.    People do not pay tithes because they do not care whether the pastors are paid or not.

**Do ye not know that they which minister about holy things live of the things of the temple? and they which wait at the altar are partakers with the altar? Even so hath the Lord ordained that they which preach the gospel should live of the gospel.**

**1 Corinthians 9:13-14**

CHURCH, IT'S TIME TO PUT AWAY CHILDISH THINGS! Do you not know that priests and pastors live off the tithes? If tithes are not paid how will the priests stay in the house of God and do their work?

But most people do not care about whether there are priests in the house of God or not. In the days of Nehemiah, the priests had left the temple and gone farming. The house of the Lord was neglected. Everyone who could be a priest had found himself a job.

Everybody wants to have a priest or a pastor for their important occasions. But most of us do not want to think about how pastors exist or what their needs are.

We just assume that they survive somehow! Not paying tithes is a declaration, "I don't care whether the church exists. I don't

41

care whether the pastors exist or not. I care about myself. As for the pastors, they will find a way to stay on the job."

**And I perceived that the portions of the Levites had not been given them: for the LEVITES AND THE SINGERS, THAT DID THE WORK, WERE FLED EVERY ONE TO HIS FIELD. Then contended I with the rulers, and said, why is the house of God forsaken? And I gathered them together, and set them in their place.**

**Nehemiah 13:10-11**

### 15.    People do not pay tithes because they have a spirit of procrastination.

**Wherefore (as the Holy Ghost saith, To day if ye will hear his voice, Harden not your hearts, as in the provocation, in the day of temptation in the wilderness:**

**Hebrews 3:7-8**

Some people have the spirit of procrastination. The spirit of procrastination says "You can do it later. You can do it tomorrow."

The most famous example of procrastination is when Moses asked Pharaoh, "WHEN SHALL I INTREAT FOR THEE, and for thy servants, and for thy people, to destroy the frogs from thee and thy houses, that they may remain in the river only? AND HE SAID, TO MORROW. And he said, Be it according to thy word: that thou mayest know that there is none like unto the Lord our God" (Exodus 8:8-10).   Pharaoh could have asked for the frogs to be removed immediately. But he asked for them to be removed the next day.  Imagine that!

Things that are not done immediately are usually not done! Many people put off their duty of tithing because it does not seem urgent. There are always more pressing bills to be paid. "I can always pay my tithes later," they say to themselves.  In the end, the tithe is pushed to the bottom of the list. And guess what? It never gets paid!

## 16.   People do not pay tithes because it has never become one of the habits of their lives.

Many people do not pay tithes because tithe paying has not become one of the habits of their lives. People have formed habits of brushing their teeth and having their baths every day. People have even formed spiritual habits of having their quiet times everyday.

Amazingly, people have not formed the habit of paying tithes regularly. Paying tithes regularly is one of the most important habits that you must develop for your life.

Many years ago, I came to the conviction that I must pay tithes regularly. I was a student in secondary school when I formed that habit. Even though I was not a salaried worker, I paid ten percent of everything I received.

Even when I was seventeen years old, I believed that not paying tithes brought about curses.

One day, a friend received her results from the exams council. She was not happy because she had not done as well as she expected to. She was not going to be able to go to the university she wanted.

She was really upset about it and we discussed the matter. I asked her whether she paid tithes. She said she did not. Then I told her with a teenager's conviction that I felt that she had not passed her exams very well because she did not pay tithes. I felt the devourer had "eaten up" some of her exam marks.

She could not believe what I was saying. She could not believe that not paying tithes could affect her exam results.

I share this experience because it reminds me of how long I have strongly believed in paying tithes. It is important to develop the good Christian habit of paying tithes as early in your life as possible.

God will bless you over the years as you faithfully support His work.

## 17.    People do not pay tithes because they think it is an Old Testament law and does not apply to them.

**Now concerning the collection for the saints, as I have given order to the churches of Galatia, even so do ye. Upon the first day of the week let every one of you lay by him in store, as God hath prospered him, that there be no gatherings when I come.**

**1 Corinthians 16:1-2**

The doctrine of tithing is found mostly in the Old Testament. But so is the doctrine of salvation. The Old Testament is as much a part of the Bible as the new. Please do not think about tithing as an archaic Old Testament law anymore because that way of thinking will destroy the basis of your Christian faith.

I love the Old Testament as much as I do the new. If you insist on thinking that tithing should be discarded because it is in the Old Testament then please do not comfort yourself with any of the Psalms any more. Do not claim any of the promises in the Psalms any more because they are from the Old Testament. Also, do not read any of the stories of Abraham, Isaac, Jacob, Joseph, Samson, Gideon, David and Goliath to your children because they are in the Old Testament. And do not forget to ignore the words of wisdom in Proverbs because those are also in the Old Testament. Dear friend, you will be committing spiritual suicide if you discarded the Old Testament and what it contains.

Remember that both Jesus and Paul taught salvation from the Scriptures. The Scriptures they taught from are what you call the Old Testament.

Every doctrine in the New Testament comes out of the Old Testament. Basing your life only on the New Testament will surely make you a lopsided and immature Christian.

True maturity comes from taking in the whole Bible and believing every Scripture in its right context. Do not say that tithing is under the law. *Tithing was before the Law, during the Law and after the Law!*

Our feet stand on solid ground when one foot is in the Old Testament and the other in the New Testament! The Old Testament is the basis for the new.

## 18. People do not pay tithes because they are suspicious and accusative.

**And they rose early in the morning, and went forth into the wilderness of Tekoa: and as they went forth, Jehoshaphat stood and said, Hear me, O Judah, and ye inhabitants of Jerusalem; Believe in the LORD your God, so shall ye be established; believe his prophets, so shall ye prosper.**

**2 Chronicles 20:20**

It is important to believe in the prophet of God who has been sent to you.

It is not difficult for pastors to recognize the untrusting and suspicious nature of some church members. They believe in God alright but they do not believe in the pastor. They suspect him of stealing money. They accuse him of using their money to live luxuriously.

They constantly discuss the pastor behind his back. They do not see why the pastor should have certain privileges. Some people in the church have an unspoken standard of living, which they expect their pastor not to cross. Most people have a mental picture of how and where they expect their pastors to live.

They reason, "After all we are sponsoring him." They always remember the phrase, "as poor as a church mouse". Anything related to the church must be poor or poverty-stricken; including the pastors. Of course, such negatively-minded people will not pay tithes.

It is important to become a positive person who believes in good things. Optimism usually breeds success. Take a room full of millionaires and business executives who have reached the pinnacle of their goals, and you will almost certainly find a room full of people who are, by their nature, optimistic and positive.

There are plenty of explanations for why that is true. Positive-minded people are achievers, and are often chosen over negative people in almost every sphere of life. A positively thinking person will pay his tithes knowing that he is using his money for a good cause.

**For as he thinketh in his heart, so is he:**
**Proverbs 23:7**

## 19.    People do not pay tithes because they are lazy.

**The slothful hideth his hand in his bosom; it grieveth him to bring it again to his mouth.**
**Proverbs 26:15**

Lazy people do not pay tithes. Many people are too lazy to bring their tithes to the church. If it is not easy or convenient to do something, they will not do it. Without intending to, many people withhold the provisions of the Levites. The priests are forced to find other means of surviving!

Many pastors are turned into thieves or extortionists because of the lack created by lazy congregants who could not be bothered to even remember that they have to tithe.

One day, I visited a church in a village outside Accra. The church building was locked. I asked the people around, "Where is the pastor?" They all laughed and murmured under their breath. In the end, I found out that the pastor had run away and abandoned the church. I also found out that this was the third pastor who had absconded.

As I looked at the surroundings of the village, I realised that the pastor had probably dashed away because he could not survive there.

There is no way to tell how many churches and ministries have closed down because there was simply not enough money to sustain the priest and keep him at post.

Do not be too lazy to pay your tithes. Do not forget this all important duty of your life. This is why God gave you the job you have and the provision that you enjoy in your life. Your failure to pay your tithes may result in the closure of an entire church.

## 20. People do not pay tithes because they are forgetful and ungrateful.

Many people do not pay tithes because they forget where they came from. They forget how God helped them to arrive at their current station. A spiritual person wants to do something to show gratitude for the grace that has lifted him to his current position. Joseph ministered to the butler. He interpreted his dream for him. But as soon as the butler was elevated he forgot all about Joseph. This is the story of many blessed people. People forget all about God when they are blessed. Forgetfulness and ungratefulness are indeed reasons why people do not pay their tithes.

**Yet did not the chief butler remember Joseph, but forgat him.**

**Genesis 40:23**

47

*Chapter 5*

# Seven Steps to Becoming Financially Useless

God has given many talents to many people. Your tithe is one of the talents God has given you. I call this the "tithing talent." The talent speaks of anything God has put in your hand. Once it is yours to use, it is a talent and you must deploy it according to the will of God.

Unfortunately, some people bury their talents and refuse to use them. Through a series of related steps, many Christians become financially useless to God. In spite of many financial endowments, Christians fail to become financially useful to the kingdom of God.

Jesus told us exactly why people hide their talents and do not use them for the service of the kingdom. Here are seven steps that explain how people deteriorate until they are financially useless in the kingdom of God.

## 1. THE FEAR OF TITHING

And I WAS AFRAID, and went and hid thy talent in the earth:

Matthew 25:25

Fear is an evil spirit which paralyses Christians into inactivity. Perhaps, it is one of the greatest forces that keep people from using their talents. At many junctions of my life, fear attempted to paralyze me into inactivity and fruitlessness. I can remember several times when fear tried to keep me from serving God and using my talents.

## 2.    HIDING THE TITHE

AND I was afraid, and WENT AND HID thy talent in the earth:

Matthew 25:25

Fear causes you to hide your tithes. Many people conceal who they are and what they can give. No one knows their potential because it is well concealed. Have you hidden your talents and gifts? Perhaps fear of criticism has caused you to hide your gifts of singing, teaching, and giving.

## 3.    A FAULT-FINDING ATTITUDE

Then he which had received the one talent came and said, LORD, I KNEW THEE THAT THOU ART AN HARD MAN, reaping where thou hast not sown, and gathering where thou hast not strawed

Matthew 25:24

The gentleman with one talent did nothing because he found fault with the master who sent him forth. He described him as a *hard man* who *benefited* from things *he did not deserve.*

Fault-finding is a common characteristic of non-tithers! Instead of getting involved in the work of God, they sit back and analyze others who are fighting hard to do something for God. It is not difficult to find fault with someone or something if you are looking for it. And what will you find about people who are striving to serve the Lord? Faults! Faults! Faults!

These faults will only become the reason for you to withhold your tithe. So why even bother to look for faults in God's servant? God did not choose angels to work for Him. He chose flaw-ridden men and women of varying backgrounds to do His work. You will always find something wrong when you look closely at God's servants. Don't look for faults. Look into the Word of God and obey it.

## 4.    DESPISING THE SMALLNESS OF YOUR TITHE

> Then he which had received THE ONE TALENT came and said, Lord, I knew thee that thou art an hard man, reaping where thou hast not sown, and gathering where thou hast not strawed: And I was afraid, and went and hid thy talent in the earth: lo, there thou hast that is thine.
>
> Matthew 25:24-25

Perhaps, the man who received one talent thought it was too small to make any significant profit. He felt it was better to do nothing than to waste his time working with only one talent. Despising your tithe because of its apparent *smallness* is one of the most dangerous spiritual mistakes you could ever make.

## 5.    NOT WANTING TO BE CHEATED

> His lord answered and said unto him, Thou wicked and slothful servant, thou knewest that I reap where I sowed not, and gather where I have not strawed:
>
> Matthew 25:26

> Let this mind be in you, which was also in Christ Jesus:Who, being in the form of God, THOUGHT IT NOT ROBBERY to be equal with God: But made himself of no reputation, and took upon him the form of a servant, and was made in the likeness of men:
>
> Philippians 2:5-7

Not wanting to be "cheated" is another important reason why people do not pay tithes. The mind that, "I am being cheated" is a thought which paralyses the average person into inaction. Many developing countries do not realise that this is the reason why they are unable to develop. The notion that rich people, or even rich countries, are cheating them prevents them from signing certain agreements that would benefit the whole country.

Just the thought that someone is cheating you will cause you to withdraw and hold back. No one likes to be cheated. Many people do not work in their churches because they feel the pastor is cheating them. This causes many talents to remain hidden and unused.

There are those who say: "Why should I go to work and give ten per cent of what I earn to this lazy pastor?"

They say, "Why should he sleep at home all week and receive ten per cent of my income? That is cheating and I will not have any of it!"

As you can see, a feeling of "being cheated" makes people inactive and hold back their tithes.

## 6.    WICKEDNESS

His lord answered and said unto him, Thou WICKED and slothful SERVANT, thou knewest that I reap where I sowed not, and gather where I have not strawed:

Matthew 25:26

The words "wicked servant" have a profound meaning; deeper than we may care to meditate on. If you do not pay the tithes that God has given you, it may cause many people to go to Hell. And that is wickedness! Avoid being called a wicked servant by giving the right portion of your income to the work of the Lord.

## 7.    BECOMING FINANCIALLY UNPROFITABLE, WORTHLESS AND USELESS

Take therefore the talent from him, and give it unto him which hath ten talents. For unto every one that hath shall be given, and he shall have abundance: but from him that hath not shall be taken away even that which he hath. And cast ye the UNPROFITABLE SERVANT into outer darkness: there shall be weeping and gnashing of teeth.

Matthew 25:28-30

At the end of this parable, Jesus declared the servant to be unprofitable, worthless and useless. Sometimes, we make the mistake of acquiring something that is useless. I once acquired a pair of shoes that were too tight. When I got home and tried them on again I realised they did not really fit me. I could not also return them because I was no longer in the country where I bought them. This beautiful pair of shoes, although expensive, became absolutely useless and worthless to me.

Has God made a mistake of saving someone like you? After He has washed you with His precious blood and made you into a new creation, have you turned out to be an unprofitable servant?

Are you useless and worthless to God?

Are you of any use when it comes to paying tithes and saving peoples lives? Please do not become one of the unprofitable and worthless Christians in your church.

*Chapter 6*

# The Bad Thoughts
# of Non-Tithers

Non-tithers become poor because their minds are full of bad thoughts. Negatively-minded people do not prosper. You need to be positive and faith-filled if you are to flourish and prosper.

**For as he thinketh in his heart, so is he:**

**Proverbs 23:7**

**Let this mind be in you, which was also in Christ Jesus:**

**Philippians 2:5**

*1.     "I earn too little to pay tithes".*

Then he which had received THE ONE TALENT came and said, Lord, I knew thee that thou art an hard man, reaping where thou hast not sown, and gathering where thou hast not strawed: And I was afraid, and went and hid thy talent in the earth: lo, there thou hast that is thine.

Matthew 25:24-25

This is a dangerous way of thinking. The Bible is replete with examples of people who were called upon to give the little they had. Those who gave of the little they had were blessed and those who didn't were cursed.

"I earn too little" is not a valid excuse in the kingdom of God. "I earn too little" is a bad thought. Remember the parable Jesus told about a man who felt he had too small a talent.

Most people in the world do not earn much or have much. And yet God requires us to give of the little that we have.

## 2. *"I earn too much to pay tithes."*

One day, I asked a brother to pay his tithes. He looked at me in amazement as if to say, "Are you mad?"

Then he asked me, "Do you know how much I earn?"

He continued, "I could never pay tithes. I earn too much to pay tithes."

You see, this brother felt that his tithes would be too large an amount to give to the church. He had no respect for the house of God.

A few years later, he was struck with an incurable disease. Faced with a hopeless situation, he turned to God and began paying tithes. I can remember the day he came to my office and said, "Pastor, I brought my tithes to church today and I wanted to specially inform you that I have begun to pay tithes."

I was happy that this brother had begun paying his tithes. But what a price to pay before we turn to God! Dear friend, there is nothing like earning too much to pay tithes. You do not earn too much to pay tithes. You earn what God has allowed you to have. To whom much is given, much is expected!

**But who am I, and what is my people, that we should be able to offer so willingly after this sort? for all things come of thee, and of thine own have we given thee.**

**1 Chronicles 29:14**

## 3.　*"I am not a fool. I will never pay tithes."*

Finally, brethren, whatsoever things are true, whatsoever things are honest, whatsoever things are just, whatsoever things are pure, whatsoever things are lovely, whatsoever things are of good report; if there be any virtue, and if there be any praise, think on these things.

Philippians 4:8

Why do you constantly think that somebody is trying to trick you? Who are you anyway? You are one of the people who thinks that pastors created the concept of the tithe to take money from people. Please give us a break! The Bible was written long before any of us was born. We did not create the concept of tithing to cheat anybody. God has shown us how to govern His church and that is exactly what we are doing.

No one thinks you are a fool. Please do not let your mind be filled with negative thoughts. We cannot have good fellowship if one party is constantly having evil thoughts about the other.

## 4.　*"My hard-earned money is not being properly used so I will not pay tithes in this church."*

LORD, my heart is not haughty, nor mine eyes lofty: neither do I exercise myself in great matters, or in things too high for me.

Psalms 131:1

There are people who think that their donations are not being properly used. Some people think that the church should go into various kinds of investments. Some people think that the church should have an insurance company. Others think that the church should own a bank. But maybe that is not the vision of your pastor. You cannot impose your ideas on the church. You can impose those ideas on your business. But you must leave the church to be governed by the pastor.

In Jewish law, according to the *tzedakah*, there are different degrees of giving. One level of giving is when you know the recipient of the money. But there is a higher level at which you give without knowing who receives the money. It is time to mature in your giving.

5.   *"The pastors are using our money to buy cars and houses for themselves so I will not pay tithes to finance their extravagant lifestyle."*

Why do you always have negative thoughts? What are you against? What are you fighting? Why do you constantly feel that your money is being used to do extravagant things for the pastor? Your thoughts are those of a poor and desperate person who thinks that other people's prosperity is the cause of your poverty.

You seem to be a  negative personality who is constantly against the privileges of leaders. Judas Iscariot did not like the privileges that were bestowed on Jesus and he said so. Do you want to be like Judas? I sense you may already be that way if you have such thoughts racing through your mind.

> Then took Mary a pound of ointment of spikenard, very costly, and anointed the feet of Jesus, and wiped his feet with her hair: and the house was filled with the odour of the ointment.
>
> Then saith one of his disciples, Judas Iscariot, Simon's son, which should betray him,
>
> Why was not this ointment sold for three hundred pence, and given to the poor?
>
> This he said, not that he cared for the poor; but because he was a thief, and had the bag, and bare what was put therein.
>
> John 12:3-6

6.   *"All pastors are con men and thieves so I will not pay tithes."*

Dear friend, you will get into serious trouble with this kind of thinking. Why do you crucify the good with the evil? Could it be that all pastors are thieves? Is this not what the Jews did to Jesus Christ? They crucified a thief and a pastor together. The good and the bad were given the same treatment.

Is that righteousness? Is it right to repay good with evil?

Woe to the man who says that an evil thing is a good thing. But also, there is a woe to the man who says that a good thing is evil.

If you keep on calling all pastors evil, you will find yourself committing a grievous sin. I wouldn't want to be around when your punishment begins to happen.

> Woe unto them that call evil good, and good evil; that put darkness for light, and light for darkness; that put bitter for sweet, and sweet for bitter!
>
> Isaiah 5:20

## 7. *"Ten percent is too much to give so I will not pay tithes."*

"Ten percent is too much, I will give five percent to God!" Why don't you tell that to the government when it is time to pay your taxes? Tell them the same thing you tell God and see if they will be happy with you.

Do you think God is a fool? Do you think He does not know the difference between ten percent and one percent? Do not belittle the Creator of the universe with such thinking. You endanger your life when you have the wrong thoughts within you.

> **Be not deceived; God is not mocked...**
>
> **Galatians 6:7**

## 8. *"I am broke so I cannot pay tithes."*

Being broke is nothing unusual. The World Bank estimated that in 2001 there were 2.7 billion classified as living below the line of moderate poverty. This figure classifies half of the world as poor, earning less than sixty dollars a month. That means that most people in the world are broke.

Being broke is not a good enough reason not to pay tithes. Not paying your tithes because you are broke is also addressed in the Bible. Most of the world is broke and most of us need extra money. But this is where priorities will be tested.

Will you put God first? Will you obey the Word of God? You have no reason to use your tithe because you are broke.

> I have not eaten thereof in my mourning, neither have I taken away ought thereof for any unclean use, nor given ought thereof for the dead: but I have hearkened to the voice of the LORD my God, and have done according to all that thou hast commanded me.
>
> Deuteronomy 26:14

> And if a man will at all redeem ought of his tithes, he shall add thereto the fifth part thereof.
>
> Leviticus 27:31

## 9. *"I am building a house so I cannot pay my tithes."*

I am sorry, but building a house is not a good enough excuse not to pay your tithes. God has never put the building of *our personal houses* before the building of *His* house.

Building God's house always comes before building your own house. God wants you to have a house. He is the one who can build it for you. Anyway, without His help, you will not live to see the completion of your house. Pay your tithes and receive a blessing on all that you do.

Avoid the curse of never completing your project!

Avoid the curse of never paying off your mortgage!

Avoid the curse of never occupying what you have built!

Avoid the curse of building only for someone else to enjoy it!

Thus speaketh the LORD of hosts, saying, This people say, The time is not come, the time that the LORD's house should be built.

Then came the word of the LORD by Haggai the prophet, saying,

Is it time for you, O ye, to dwell in your ceiled houses, and this house lie waste?

Now therefore thus saith the LORD of hosts; Consider your ways.

Ye have sown much, and bring in little; ye eat, but ye have not enough; ye drink, but ye are not filled with drink; ye clothe you, but there is none warm; and he that earneth wages earneth wages to put it into a bag with holes.

Haggai 1:2-6

## 10. *"I have a funeral to fund so I cannot pay tithes this month."*

Why don't you tell the government that you have a funeral to finance so you will not pay your taxes this month? Why don't you tell your children that you have a funeral to fund so you will not pay their school fees this term? Why don't you tell your wife that you have a funeral to fund so you will not pay the utility bills? Why don't you tell yourself that you have a funeral to finance so you will not eat this month?

Why do you always think of God's holy tithe as the first thing you can drop? Does it show respect for God? I do not think so. Funeral expenses and emergencies are not good enough reasons to not pay tithes.

I have not eaten thereof in my mourning, neither have I taken away ought thereof for any unclean use, nor given ought thereof for the dead: but I have hearkened to the voice of the LORD my God, and have done according to all that thou hast commanded me.

Deuteronomy 26:14

## 11.    *"I have a lot of debts so I cannot pay tithes."*

Most people in the world are in one form of debt or the other. Why do you treat your tithes as a beard that can be shaved off? Why do you put God's work after everything you do? Is it a nice thing to do?

I watched a film in which Rambo was asked why he had been sent on such a dangerous mission. He answered, "Because I am expendable." That was a sad moment in the film because of the emotion created by the feeling of him being expendable.

You see, when you are expendable it means you are non-essential. To many people, paying tithes is non-essential! They treat their commitment to God as something unneeded and unwanted.

Do you think God does not notice your attitude towards Him and His work? Continue to treat God as non-essential and you will see what will happen to you!!

## 12.    *"I am a widow so I cannot pay tithes."*

I would agree with you that widows are to be pitied and helped. It would seem even cruel for a widow to give away some of her little money. However, giving money away and paying tithes is not meant to be something rational. The spiritual truths are unchanged. If you sow, you will reap. A widow needs to reap much more than an ordinary person.

Do you remember the widow who cast in two mites? Why didn't Jesus send her away and say, "She is too poor to give an offering?" "And Jesus sat over against the treasury, and beheld how the people cast money into the treasury: and many that were rich cast in much. And there came a certain poor widow, and she threw in two mites, which make a farthing. And he called unto him his disciples, and saith unto them, Verily I say unto you, That this poor widow hath cast more in, than all they which have cast into the treasury" (Mark 12:41-43)

Do you remember when Elijah told the widow to make him some bread with her last dregs of oil and flour? Was Elijah a cruel, heartless man of God, taking things from the poorest of the poor? Certainly not! He was opening a door for the blessing to come into the widow's life. Do not use your widowhood as a reason for not paying tithes. You will be missing out on a great blessing if you do not pay tithes.

### 13. "I am a student so I cannot pay tithes."

Being a student must not prevent you from paying tithes. Do students eat food? Do students wear clothes? Do students drive cars? Do students have money? Do students get married? The answers to all these questions is YES! How come students are able to engage in all the things I have listed above?

Do you know that many students think that they are wiser than adults? If students are wiser than adults, why can't they pay tithes?

I am sorry; I cannot let you off because you are a student.

You must pay your tithes! If you don't pay tithes then you must equally stop all these other activities which students do. Students are able-bodied young men and women who receive an income of some sort. Students have substance and they must honour the Lord with their substance! Students have substance and they must honour God with it!

Honour the LORD with thy substance, and with the firstfruits of all thine increase:

Proverbs 3:9

### 14. "I am unemployed so I cannot pay tithes."

Thank you for telling us that you are unemployed! We didn't know about your situation. But I have a question for you: Do you eat everyday? Do you have clothes to wear? Do you go out? Do you travel? Where do you get money for all these things?

Please do not throw dust into our eyes by saying that you are unemployed and cannot pay tithes. I think you want to use your unemployed status as a smokescreen. You want to hide behind that screen and use it as an excuse for not paying tithes.

**He that is faithful in that which is least is faithful also in much: and he that is unjust in the least is unjust also in much.**

**Luke 16:10**

Many, many people in this world have no jobs. But one way or another, they are sustained in this world.

Your time of being unemployed is the time of having little. The Word of God is encouraging you to be faithful with little. In the day you are employed you will have much more. If you are faithful with the little you will be faithful with much.

Everyone has two phases in his life: the phase of employment and the phase of unemployment. You are expected to pay tithes in the unemployed phase as well as the employed phase of your life. I have paid tithes for the last thirty years of my life. Ten out of those thirty years, I was unemployed. Yet it never occurred to me that I should not pay my tithes because I did not have a job.

## 15. *"I am retired and on pension so I cannot and will not pay tithes."*

It is good to know that you are retired. But even retirees live, eat, drink, wear clothes and go in and out every day. Sometimes, retirees have even more money than active workers. Just remember that older people are supposed to set an example for the younger. Please show us the way by being a good example and paying tithes of all that God provides for you through your pension, your investments, your savings, your gifts and your children.

## 16. "I give my money to help the poor and to do other humanitarian projects so I do not need to pay tithes."

God bless you for your contributions to help other humanitarian projects. It is a great blessing and you will be rewarded for that. But remember the words of Jesus when He said,

**...these ought ye to have done, and not to leave the other undone.**

**Matthew 23:23**

Help the poor, help the blind, feed the hungry! But pay your tithes as well. Do not leave tithe paying undone. Church, it's time to put away childish things, the tithe belongs to the church!

## 17. "I don't want anyone to know how much I earn so I will not pay tithes."

Why do you think you are so important? Why do you think that everybody is trying to find out how much you earn? First of all, your mind is not working correctly. Secondly, there are many people who know your income including your bank, your workplace, your colleagues, your social security office and the tax office. How come all these people know what you earn but it is not a problem to you? How come you don't want anyone at the church to know what you earn?

Anyway, if you really do not want people to know what you earn, you can camouflage your giving and give in such a way that no one can determine exactly how much you earn. Just make sure you give what you are supposed to so that you will be blessed.

Please do not create imaginary obstacles for paying tithes which are neither substantial nor real.

## 18. "I have never paid tithes and I do not see any curses in my life so I will not pay tithes."

You have revealed your spiritual shallowness by this statement. God told Adam: *"...in the day that you eat [from the tree] you shall surely die"* (Genesis 2:17). But did he die physically? Did he not continue to live on and even have children afterwards? Even though he did not die physically on that day, we all know that a great curse of death fell on Adam and his descendants. Be careful with such irresponsible thoughts. You may get yourself into serious trouble.

> Ye have said, It is vain to serve God: and what profit is it that we have kept his ordinance, and that we have walked mournfully before the LORD of hosts?

> Malachi 3:14

## 19. "When I pay my tithes I do not see any financial improvements in my life so I will not pay tithes."

God is not a robot or a computer. Serving God is not the same as using your computer where commands are given, buttons are pressed and things happen. God has never reduced himself to the level of a computer and He will not. He has promised to pour out his blessings on those who pay tithes.

If you do not see any financial blessings in your life, then I suggest you read the chapter in which I share many reasons about why you may not experience financial increase even though you pay tithes. Never forget that all things work together for good. Many things work together to bring the good results we desire.

> **Ye have said, It is vain to serve God: and what profit is it that we have kept his ordinance, and that we have walked mournfully before the LORD of hosts?**

> **Malachi 3:14**

## Chapter 7

# Prophetic Warnings against Forgetting God and Not Tithing

After the law was given by Moses, the children of Israel went right ahead and broke most of these laws. The prophetic books contain so many warnings of impending judgement that you get the impression that God just wants to kill, punish and burn His people.

This is an unfortunate impression that many people have of the Lord.

How would you feel if you provided everything for your children who then referred to someone else as the source of all that they have? How would you feel if you were constantly forgotten and forsaken by the very ones you had blessed so much?

The following prophetic pronouncements were made against the children of Israel because they forgot the source of their blessing. The Lord showed them how He had provided their silver, gold, grain and wine. Yet they did not even know it or acknowledge it. Their gratitude was directed towards false gods who had nothing to do with their prosperity. Notice the severe punishment determined for people who forget the source of their blessings. Three prophets, Hosea, Jeremiah and Isaiah, warn the people not to forget the source of their blessings.

This is a warning that applies to us today. The Christians of today have experienced a level of prosperity and provision that no other generation has enjoyed. And yet Christians today have forgotten their God and the source of their blessings. It is time to return to God. It is time to honour the Lord for all that He has given us. If we indeed refuse to become grateful, tithing Christians we will fall into the same curses that the Israelite nation fell into. Notice the warnings of these three prophets. These are also warnings to this generation of believers.

## 1. The Prophetic Warnings of Hosea to Prosperous Believers

FOR SHE DOES NOT KNOW THAT IT WAS I WHO GAVE HER THE GRAIN, THE NEW WINE AND THE OIL, AND LAVISHED ON HER SILVER AND GOLD, WHICH THEY USED FOR BAAL.

THEREFORE, I WILL TAKE BACK MY GRAIN AT HARVEST TIME AND MY NEW WINE IN ITS SEASON. I will also take away My wool and My flax given to cover her nakedness.

And then I will uncover her lewdness in the sight of her lovers, and no one will rescue her out of My hand.

I will also put an end to all her gaiety, her feasts, her new moons, her sabbaths

And all her festal assemblies.

I will destroy her vines and fig trees, of which she said, ' These are my wages which my lovers have given me.'

And I will make them a forest, and the beasts of the field will devour them.

I will punish her for the days of the Baals when she used to offer sacrifices to them and adorn herself with her earrings and jewelry, and follow her lovers, so that SHE FORGOT ME," DECLARES THE LORD.

Hosea 2:8-13 (NASB)

## 2.     The Prophetic Warnings of Jeremiah to Forgetful Believers

SURELY AS A WIFE TREACHEROUSLY DEPARTETH FROM HER HUSBAND, SO HAVE YE DEALT TREACHEROUSLY WITH ME, O house of Israel, saith the LORD.

A voice was heard upon the high places, weeping and supplications of the children of Israel: for they have perverted their way, AND THEY HAVE FORGOTTEN THE LORD THEIR GOD.

Return, ye backsliding children, and I will heal your backslidings. Behold, we come unto thee; for thou art the LORD our God.

Jeremiah 3:20-22

## 3.     The Prophetic Warnings of Isaiah for the People to Bring their Offerings to the Lord

Behold, I will do a new thing; now it shall spring forth; shall ye not know it? I will even make a way in the wilderness, and rivers in the desert.

67

The beast of the field shall honour me, the dragons and the owls: because I give waters in the wilderness, and rivers in the desert, to give drink to my people, my chosen.

This people have I formed for myself; they shall shew forth my praise.

BUT THOU HAST NOT CALLED UPON ME, O JACOB; BUT THOU HAST BEEN WEARY OF ME, O ISRAEL.

THOU HAST NOT BROUGHT ME THE SMALL CATTLE OF THY BURNT OFFERINGS; NEITHER HAST THOU HONOURED ME WITH THY SACRIFICES. I have not caused thee to serve with an offering, nor wearied thee with incense.

Thou hast bought me no sweet cane with money, neither hast thou filled me with the fat of thy sacrifices: but thou hast made me to serve with thy sins, thou hast wearied me with thine iniquities.

Isaiah 43:19-24

# Section 2

# How Tithing Christians
# Can Become Rich

*Chapter 8*

# Seven Things Every Christian Should Know about the Tithe

1.  *Dekate* **is the Greek word which is translated into the word "tithe" and means "the tenth" or "ten percent" of everything that you have.**

2.  **The tithe is the firstfruits of everything that you have.**

T he word "tithe" is used interchangeably with the word "firstfruits" and there are several examples of this in the Bible. This is important because the word "firstfruits" is more commonly used in New Testament language. Because the word firstfruits is more commonly used in the New Testament church, some people erroneously assume that the concept of tithing is a Jewish Old Testament practice, which does not apply today. Notice four examples of how the word "tithe" is interchanged with the word "firstfruits" in the Old Testament. This proves that the tithe is the same as the firstfruit.

**a. Nehemiah referred to the tithe as first fruits. Nehemiah used the terms tithes and first fruits interchangeably.**

Also that day they offered great sacrifices, and rejoiced: for God had made them rejoice with great joy: the wives also and the children rejoiced: so that the joy of Jerusalem was heard even afar off.

And at that time were some appointed over the chambers for the treasures, for the offerings, for THE FIRSTFRUITS, and for THE TITHES, to gather into them out of the fields of the cities the portions of the law for the priests and Levites: for Judah rejoiced for the priests and for the Levites that waited.

Nehemiah 12:43-44

And to bring the FIRSTFRUITS of our ground, and the FIRSTFRUITS of all fruit of all trees, year by year, unto the house of the LORD:

Also the firstborn of our sons, and of our cattle, as it is written in the law, and the FIRSTLINGS of our herds and of our flocks, to bring to the house of our God, unto the priests that minister in the house of our God:

And that we should bring the FIRSTFRUITS of our dough, and our offerings, and the fruit of all manner of trees, of wine and of oil, unto the priests, to the chambers of the house of our God; and the TITHES of our ground unto the Levites, that the same Levites might have the TITHES in all the cities of our tillage.

Nehemiah 10:35-37

**b. Ezekiel described the tithes for the priests as "firstfruits".**

The first of all the first fruits of every kind and every contribution of every kind, from all your contributions, shall be for the priests; you shall also give to the priest the first of your dough to cause a blessing to rest on your house.

Ezekiel 44:30 (NASB)

**c. Hezekiah referred to the tithe as firstfruits. Hezekiah used the terms tithes and firstfruits interchangeably.**

Now when all this was finished, all Israel that were present went out to the cities of Judah, and brake the images in pieces, and cut down the groves, and threw down the high places and the altars out of all Judah and Benjamin, in Ephraim also and Manasseh, until they had utterly destroyed them all. Then all the children of Israel returned, every man to his possession, into their own cities.

And Hezekiah appointed the courses of the priests and the Levites after their courses, every man according to his service, the priests and Levites for burnt offerings and for peace offerings, to minister, and to give thanks, and to praise in the gates of the tents of the Lord.

He appointed also the king's portion of his substance for the burnt offerings, to wit, for the morning and evening burnt offerings, and the burnt offerings for the sabbaths, and for the new moons, and for the set feasts, as it is written in the law of the Lord.

Moreover he commanded the people that dwelt in Jerusalem to give THE PORTION OF THE PRIESTS AND THE LEVITES, that they might be encouraged in the law of the Lord.

And as soon as the commandment came abroad, the children of Israel brought in abundance the FIRSTFRUITS OF CORN, wine, and oil, and honey, and of all the increase of the fields; and the TITHE OF ALL THINGS brought they in abundantly.

And concerning the children of Israel and Judah, that dwelt in the cities of Judah, they also brought in the TITHE OF OXEN and sheep, and the TITHE OF HOLY THINGS which were consecrated unto the Lord their God, and laid them by heaps.

2 Chronicles 31:1-6

**d. Solomon described the tithes to be presented as firstfruits.**

Honour the Lord with thy substance, and with THE FIRSTFRUITS OF ALL THINE INCREASE: so shall thy barns be filled with plenty, and thy presses shall burst out with new wine.

Proverbs 3:9-10

**3.    The tithe is God's property.   It is money that actually belongs to God.**

And all THE TITHE of the land, whether of the seed of the land, or of the fruit of the tree, IS THE LORD'S: it is holy unto the Lord.

Leviticus 27:30

**4.    The tithe is holy money and anyone that misuses it misuses a holy thing.**

And all THE TITHE of the land, whether of the seed of the land, or of the fruit of the tree, is the Lord's: IT IS HOLY UNTO THE LORD.

Leviticus 27:30

**5.    The tithe is used to support the priests.**

Neither must the children of Israel henceforth come nigh the tabernacle of the congregation, lest they bear sin, and die.

But the Levites shall do the service of the tabernacle of the congregation, and they shall bear their iniquity: it shall be a statute for ever throughout your generations, that among the children of Israel they have no inheritance.

But THE TITHES OF THE CHILDREN OF ISRAEL, which they offer as an heave offering unto the Lord, I HAVE GIVEN TO THE LEVITES TO INHERIT: therefore I have said unto them, Among the children of Israel they shall have no inheritance. And the LORD spake unto Moses, saying,

Thus speak unto the Levites, and say unto them, When ye take of the children of Israel the tithes which I have given you from them for your inheritance, then ye shall offer up an heave offering of it for the LORD, even a tenth part of the tithe. And this your heave offering shall be reckoned unto you, as though it were the corn of the threshingfloor, and as the fulness of the winepress. Thus ye also shall offer an heave offering unto the LORD of all your tithes, which ye receive of the children of Israel; and ye shall give thereof the LORD'S heave offering to Aaron the priest. Out of all your gifts ye shall offer every heave offering of the LORD, of all the best thereof, even the hallowed part thereof out of it. Therefore thou shalt say unto them, When ye have heaved the best thereof from it, then it shall be counted unto the Levites as the increase of the threshingfloor, and as the increase of the winepress. AND YE SHALL EAT IT in every place, ye and your households: FOR IT IS YOUR REWARD FOR YOUR SERVICE IN THE TABERNACLE of the congregation. AND YE SHALL BEAR NO SIN BY REASON OF IT, when ye have heaved from it the best of it: neither shall ye pollute the holy things of the children of Israel, lest ye die.

Numbers 18:22-32

## 6.    There are seven different types of tithes.

### Seven Types of Tithes

a.    A tithe of the flocks and herds of sheep and oxen

And concerning the children of Israel and Judah, that dwelt in the cities of Judah, they also brought in THE TITHE OF OXEN AND SHEEP, and the tithe of holy things which were consecrated unto the Lord their God, and laid them by heaps.

2 Chronicles 31: 6

And concerning the TITHE OF THE HERD, or OF THE FLOCK, even of whatsoever passeth under the rod, the tenth shall be holy unto the Lord.

Leviticus 27:32

### b. A tithe of their fruits from the fields

And all THE TITHE of the land, whether of the seed of the land, or OF THE FRUIT of the tree, is the Lord's: it is holy unto the Lord.

Leviticus 27:30

### c. A tithe of their industries which produced oil, wine, and corn

Then brought all Judah the tithe of the corn and the new wine and the oil unto the treasuries.

Nehemiah 13:12

### d. A tithe of the smallest possessions

Woe unto you, scribes and Pharisees, hypocrites! for ye pay tithe of mint and anise and cummin, and have omitted the weightier matters of the law, judgment, mercy, and faith: these ought ye to have done, and not to leave the other undone.

Matthew 23:23

### e. A tithe of their profits

At the end of three years thou shalt bring forth all THE TITHE OF THINE INCREASE the same year, and shalt lay it up within thy gates:

Deuteronomy 14:28

## f.   A tithe of their children

And to bring the firstfruits of our ground, and the firstfruits of all fruit of all trees, year by year, unto the house of the Lord: ALSO THE FIRSTBORN OF OUR SONS, and of our cattle, as it is written in the law, and the firstlings of our herds and of our flocks, to bring to the house of our God, UNTO THE PRIESTS THAT MINISTER IN THE HOUSE OF OUR GOD:

And that we should bring the firstfruits of our dough, and our offerings, and the fruit of all manner of trees, of wine and of oil, unto the priests, to the chambers of the house of our God; and the tithes of our ground unto the Levites, that the same Levites might have the tithes in all the cities of our tillage.

Nehemiah 10:35-37

## g.   A tithe of the tithe

And the Lord spake unto Moses, saying, thus speak unto the Levites, and say unto them, When ye take of the children of Israel the tithes which I have given you from them for your inheritance, then ye shall offer up an heave offering of it for the Lord, EVEN A TENTH PART OF THE TITHE.

Numbers 18:25-26

## 7.   If ever the tithe is used, it must be replaced with interest.

And all the tithe of the land, whether of the seed of the land, or of the fruit of the tree, is the Lord's: it is holy unto the Lord. And if a man will at all redeem ought of his tithes, he shall add thereto the fifth part thereof.

Leviticus 27:30-31

## Chapter 9

# Why God Established the Tithe

## The Mysterious Purposes of the Tithe

The tithe is a mysterious multi-purpose offering that is presented to the house of the Lord. Your tithe mysteriously achieves numerous purposes of God. Every time you pay tithes, you contribute towards one of these mysterious purposes. When you contribute towards each of these purposes, God unlocks a different type of blessing. You may not have intended to directly accomplish any of these things but you will indirectly contribute towards them every time you pay tithes.

In this chapter, I want you to understand the mysterious purposes of the tithe as outlined by the prophet Moses.

**1.    God established the tithe for people to show gratitude to God.**

And it shall be, WHEN THOU ART COME IN UNTO THE

LAND WHICH THE LORD THY GOD GIVETH THEE for an inheritance, and possessest it, and dwellest therein; that thou shalt take of the first of all the fruit of the earth, which thou shalt bring of thy land that the Lord thy God giveth thee, and shalt put it in a basket, and shalt go unto the place which the Lord thy God shall choose to place his name there. And thou shalt go unto the priest that shall be in those days, and say unto him, I profess this day unto the Lord thy God, that I am come unto the country which the Lord sware unto our fathers for to give us.

Deuteronomy 26:1-3

**2. God established the tithe for people to remember where God lifted them from.**

And the priest shall take the basket out of thine hand, and set it down before the altar of the Lord thy God.

And thou shalt speak and say before the Lord thy God, A SYRIAN READY TO PERISH WAS MY FATHER, and he went down into Egypt, and sojourned there with a few, and became there a nation, great, mighty, and populous: and the Egyptians evil entreated us, and afflicted us, and laid upon us hard bondage:

Deuteronomy 26:4-6

**3. God established the tithe as a prayer of thanksgiving.**

And when we cried unto the Lord God of our fathers, the Lord heard our voice, and looked on our affliction, and our labour, and our oppression:

And the Lord brought us forth out of Egypt with a mighty hand, and with an outstretched arm, and with great terribleness, and with signs, and with wonders:

And he hath brought us into this place, and hath given us this land, even a land that floweth with milk and honey.

And now, behold, I have brought the firstfruits of the land, which thou, O Lord, hast given me. AND THOU SHALT SET IT BEFORE THE LORD THY GOD, AND WORSHIP BEFORE THE LORD thy God:

Deuteronomy 26:7-10

**4.      God established the tithe so that you would enjoy the ninety percent knowing that you have given God His due.**

And thou shalt rejoice in every good thing which the Lord thy God hath given unto thee, and unto thine house, thou, and the Levite, and the stranger that is among you.

Deuteronomy 26:11

**5.      God established the tithe to pay the pastors (Levites) and keep them working in the house of God.**

When thou hast made an end of tithing all the tithes of thine increase the third year, which is the year of tithing, AND HAST GIVEN IT UNTO THE LEVITE, the stranger, the fatherless, and the widow, that they may eat within thy gates, and be filled;

Deuteronomy 26:12

**6.      God established the tithe to care for the needy and the helpless.**

Then thou shalt say before the Lord thy God, I have brought away the hallowed things out of mine house, and also have given them unto the Levite, AND UNTO THE STRANGER, TO THE FATHERLESS, AND TO THE WIDOW, according to all thy commandments which thou hast commanded me: I have not transgressed thy commandments, neither have I forgotten them:

Deuteronomy 26:13

## 7. God established the tithe as money set apart from all secular or worldly purposes.

I have not eaten thereof in my mourning, NEITHER HAVE I TAKEN AWAY OUGHT THEREOF FOR ANY UNCLEAN USE, nor given ought thereof for the dead: but I have hearkened to the voice of the Lord my God, and have done according to all that thou hast commanded me.

Deuteronomy 26:14

## 8. God established the tithe to have a legal basis to bless His people.

Look down from thy holy habitation, from heaven, and BLESS THY PEOPLE ISRAEL, and the land which thou hast given us, as thou swarest unto our fathers, a land that floweth with milk and honey.

Deuteronomy 26:15

## 9. God established the tithe as a test of our obedience.

This day the Lord thy God hath commanded thee to do these statutes and judgments: THOU SHALT THEREFORE KEEP AND DO THEM WITH ALL THINE HEART, AND WITH ALL THY SOUL.

Thou hast avouched the Lord this day to be thy God, and to walk in his ways, and to keep his statutes, and his commandments, and his judgments, and to hearken unto his voice:

Deuteronomy 26:16-17

10.   **God established the tithe in order to create a peculiar and unusual group of prosperous and blessed people on the earth.   This is what has happened to the Jews.**

And the Lord hath avouched thee this day to be his peculiar people, as he hath promised thee, and that thou shouldest keep all his commandments;

AND TO MAKE THEE HIGH ABOVE ALL NATIONS WHICH HE HATH MADE, IN PRAISE, AND IN NAME, AND IN HONOUR; and that thou mayest be an holy people unto the Lord thy God, as he hath spoken.

Deuteronomy 26:18-19

*Chapter 10*

# Seven Pioneers
# of Tithing

Throughout the Bible, many different people practised tithing. You will notice that each of these people was very different, but demonstrated some principles of tithing. Also, each of these biblical pioneers of tithing highlighted different aspects of tithing. In this chapter, I want you to discover what each of them contributed to the doctrine and practice of tithing.

## Six Things Abraham Taught Us about Tithing

1.  **Abraham showed that tithing was practised long before the laws of Moses were instituted.**

2.  **Abraham showed that tithing was not a law that had to be obeyed, but a practice that common sense should lead you to.**

3.  **Abraham showed that tithes were to be paid to the priests.**

4.     **Abraham showed that paying tithes to the priest led to more blessings.**

5.     **Abraham showed that tithing can be practised by very rich people.** "And Abram was very rich in cattle, in silver, and in gold" (Genesis 13:2).

6.     **Abraham showed us that priests are greater than rich men because the lesser is always blessed of the greater.** Abraham was a rich man and Melchizedek was a priest. But it was Melchizedek who blessed Abraham and not vice versa.

And the king of Sodom went out to meet him after his return from the slaughter of Chedorlaomer, and of the kings that were with him, at the valley of Shaveh, which is the king's dale.

And Melchizedek king of Salem brought forth bread and wine: and he was the priest of the most high God.

And he blessed him, and said, blessed be Abram of the most high God, possessor of heaven and earth: and blessed be the most high God, which hath delivered thine enemies into thy hand. And he gave him tithes of all.

Genesis 14:17-20

NOW OBSERVE HOW GREAT THIS MAN WAS TO WHOM ABRAHAM, THE PATRIARCH, GAVE A TENTH OF THE CHOICEST SPOILS.

And those indeed of the sons of Levi who receive the priest's office have commandment in the Law to collect a tenth from the people, that is, from their brethren, although these are descended from Abraham.

But the one whose genealogy is not traced from them collected a tenth from Abraham and blessed the one who had the promises.

BUT WITHOUT ANY DISPUTE THE LESSER IS BLESSED BY THE GREATER.

In this case mortal men receive tithes, but in that case one receives them, of whom it is witnessed that he lives on.

And, so to speak, through Abraham even Levi, who received tithes, paid tithes, for he was still in the loins of his father when Melchizedek met him.

Hebrews 7:4-10 (NASB)

## Four Things Moses Taught Us about Tithing

1.  **Moses showed us how the tithe actually belonged to the Lord.**

2.  **Moses taught us that the primary use of the tithe was for the sustenance of the priests' work.**

3.  **Moses taught us that the tithe was the inheritance and provision for ministers of God.**

4.  **Moses taught us that the priest must also offer a tithe of what he receives.**

And the Lord spake unto Moses, saying,

Thus speak unto the Levites, and say unto them, When ye take of the children of Israel the TITHES which I have given you from them for your inheritance, then ye shall offer up an heave offering of it for the Lord, even a tenth part of the TITHE.

And this your heave offering shall be reckoned unto you, as though it were the corn of the threshingfloor, and as the fulness of the winepress.

Thus YE ALSO SHALL OFFER AN HEAVE OFFERING UNTO THE LORD OF ALL YOUR TITHES, WHICH YE

RECEIVE OF THE CHILDREN OF ISRAEL; and ye shall give thereof the Lord's heave offering to Aaron the priest.

Out of all your gifts ye shall offer every heave offering of the Lord, of all the best thereof, even the hallowed part thereof out of it.

Numbers 18:25-29

## Six Things Solomon Taught Us about Tithing

1.  **Solomon taught us that tithes were first fruits, which meant that the first thing to be done with money is to pay tithes.**

2.  **Solomon taught us that tithes must be paid on the profit that God gives.**

3.  **Solomon taught us that tithing is our way of honouring God.**

4.  **Solomon taught us that our substance can be used to honour God.**

5.  **Solomon taught that tithing leads to abundance.**

6.  **Solomon taught that tithing leads to bursting, overflowing prosperity.**

Honour the Lord with thy substance, and with the firstfruits of all thine increase:

So shall thy barns be filled with plenty, and thy presses shall burst out with new wine.

Proverbs 3:9-10

## What Jacob Taught Us about Tithing

1.  **Jacob showed that people who pay tithes have had a deep spiritual encounter with God.** It was only after

Jacob had a personal spiritual encounter with God that he started paying tithes. People who do not pay tithes are often unspiritual men.

2.   **Jacob taught that tithing was a way of showing gratitude to God for His protection and His provision.**

3.   **Jacob showed that tithing was a personal covenant with God for protection and prosperity.**

And Jacob vowed a vow, saying, IF GOD WILL BE WITH ME, and will keep me in this way that I go, and will give me bread to eat, and raiment to put on, So that I come again to my father's house in peace; then shall the Lord be my God: And this stone, which I have set for a pillar, shall be God's house: and of all that thou shalt give me I WILL SURELY GIVE THE TENTH UNTO THEE.

Genesis 28:20-22

# What Nehemiah Taught Us about Tithing

1.   **Nehemiah showed us the need for people to pay their tithes to prevent priests from abandoning their calling.**

2.   **Nehemiah showed that the house of God was forsaken when people did not pay tithes.**

3.   **Nehemiah showed that when one person understood the importance of the tithe there could be a great revival.**

And I came to Jerusalem, and understood of the evil that Eliashib did for Tobiah, in preparing him a chamber in the courts of the house of God.

And it grieved me sore: therefore I cast forth all the household stuff of Tobiah out of the chamber.

Then I commanded, and they cleansed the chambers: and thither brought I again the vessels of the house of God, with the meat offering and the frankincense.

And I PERCEIVED THAT THE PORTIONS OF THE LEVITES HAD NOT BEEN GIVEN THEM: FOR THE LEVITES AND THE SINGERS, THAT DID THE WORK, WERE FLED EVERY ONE TO HIS FIELD.

Then contended I with the rulers, and said, why is the house of God forsaken? And I gathered them together, and set them in their place.

Then brought all Judah the TITHE of the corn and the new wine and the oil unto the treasuries.

Nehemiah 13:7-12

## What the Pharisees Taught Us about Tithing

1. **The Pharisees showed us that tithing is indeed a form of righteousness.**

2. **The Pharisees showed us that tithing and fasting are similar spiritual activities.**

3. **The Pharisees showed us that you must not become proud because you pay your tithes faithfully.**

4. **The Pharisees showed us that you may pay your tithes but still not please God.**

And he spake this parable unto certain which trusted in themselves that THEY WERE RIGHTEOUS, and despised others:

Two men went up into the temple to pray; the one a Pharisee, and the other a publican.

The Pharisee stood and prayed thus with himself, God, I thank thee, that I am not as other men are, extortioners, unjust, adulterers, or even as this publican.

I fast twice in the week, I give tithes of all that I possess.

And the publican, standing afar off, would not lift up so much as his eyes unto heaven, but smote upon his breast, saying, God be merciful to me a sinner.

I tell you, this man went down to his house justified rather than the other: for every one that exalteth himself shall be abased; and he that humbleth himself shall be exalted.

Luke 18:9-14

## What Jesus Taught Us about Tithing

1.  **Jesus showed us that tithing is not considered a "weighty" aspect of the law.**

2.  **Jesus showed us that if a Christian is unable to tithe, he is disobeying the lesser aspects of God's commandments and is therefore more likely to disobey weightier laws.**

3.  **Jesus showed us that even though we may fulfil the weightier matters of the law we must still pay tithes**

WOE UNTO YOU, Scribes and Pharisees, hypocrites! for YE PAY TITHE OF MINT AND ANISE AND CUMMIN, AND HAVE OMITTED THE WEIGHTIER MATTERS of the law, judgment, mercy, and faith: these ought ye to have done, and not to leave the other undone.

Matthew 23:23

*Chapter 11*

# The Legendary
# Wealth of Jews

I had heard about the legendary wealth of Jews and always wondered whether it was so. I was happy to discover these facts that prove that their wealth is more than a myth. It is a reality that Jews stand out as a small group of persecuted people who are generally wealthier than other ethnic groups.

Mark Twain once wrote:

- The Jews constitute but one percent of the human race. Properly the Jew ought hardly to be heard of; but he is heard of, has always been heard of.

- He is a successful businessman, the immense wholesale business of Broadway is substantially in his hands.

- Eighty-five percent of the great and lucrative businesses of Germany are in the hands of the Jewish race. The Jew is a money-getter.[1]

In reality, Jews do not constitute even one tenth of one percent of the human race. Mark Twain may have grossly overestimated the size of the world's Jewish population, but he was quite right to observe that Jews are disproportionately successful in business. From notorious Nazis to Hassidic scholars, from Japan's cultural commentators to conspiracy theorists who have never met a Jew, all who have examined the historic and current identity of the Jewish people acknowledge one simple truth – Jews are good at business.

This is true not only in the United States of the twenty-first century, but also in many countries over many centuries.

- Whether in Europe, North Africa, or the United States, Jews have always been both reviled and admired.

- Jews are hated and envied; they are despised and loved.

- For people that make up only a little over two percent of the U.S. population, they are disproportionately influential in so many areas of American life.

- They are spoken of, written about, and depicted far more than other groups of similar size. Part of the reason for this is surely their conspicuous economic success.

## Nine Facts about the Wealth of Jews

1. The percentage of Jewish households with income greater than $50,000 is double that of non-Jews.

2. The percentage of Jewish households with income less than $20,000 is half that of non-Jews.

3. The Jewish advantage in economic status persists to the present day; it remains higher than that of white Protestants and Catholics, even among households of similar age, composition and location."

4. Forty-five percent of the top 40 of the Forbes 400 richest Americans are Jewish.

5. One-third of American multimillionaires are tallied as Jewish.

6. Twenty percent of professors at leading universities are Jewish.

7.    Forty percent of partners in the leading law firms in New York and Washington are Jewish.

8.    Thirty percent of American Nobel prize winners in science and 25 percent of all American Nobel winners are Jewish.

9.    Dr Thomas Sowell, an African-American economist and senior fellow at the Hoover Institute, created a point scale index that graphed Jewish economic success compared with that of other ethnic groups.[2]

## Ethnic Household Income within the United States.

| | |
|---|---|
| US Avg. | 100 |
| Jewish | 172 |
| Japanese | 132 |
| Polish | 115 |
| Chinese | 112 |
| Italian | 112 |
| German | 107 |
| Anglo-Saxon | 107 |
| Irish | 103 |
| Filipino | 99 |
| West Indian | 94 |
| Mexican | 76 |
| Puerto Rican | 63 |
| Black | 32 |
| Native American | 60 [3] |

# What Are the Secrets to Such Phenomenal Wealth?

No doubt about it, the statistics of Jewish success – especially given the relatively small Jewish population – are remarkable. Of course, there are always individual exceptions to a general rule, just as individuals will vary within any group. However, when we view the complete picture, we see a big Jewish difference, and there must be some reasons for it.

What secrets to success have the Jews learned that can apply to any life, any family and any community?

The research held the answer. A wealth of literature and data that chronicles the lives of Jewish people throughout the ages provides the clues. Countless individual Jewish success stories led to the discovery of seven core values of beliefs that lay at the heart of Jewish achievement. In various combinations, these secrets have contributed significantly to the economic success of the Jewish people.[4]

*Chapter 12*

# Secrets to the Wealth of Jews

## The Religious Foundation of Jews

Different books have outlined what they believe to be the keys to the wealth of Jews. I do not doubt that these keys have contributed to the wealth of the Jews. However, I am particularly interested in references made to *what I believe is the real root of Jewish wealth*. I believe that Jews have followed the principles of tithing and giving more than any other group of people. To me, this is the single factor that lies at the heart of their wealth. Let's look at some of the beliefs that Jews have.

What makes Jews different from other ethnic groups is a specific religious culture that has shaped their values and strongly influenced how they view the world.

The beliefs of Jews are taken from different holy books including: the *Mishna*, the *Talmud* and the *Torah*. Their lives are regulated by these beliefs and thousands of years have not eroded the fundamentals of what they believe about God and man.

# The Jewish Holy Books

**Mishna**: is a collection of books that outlines the detailed laws for daily Jewish living. It is also the teaching of a Rabbi or other noted authority on Jewish laws.

**The Talmud**: is a vast collection of Jewish laws and traditions and consists of a rabbinical commentary on the Old Testament.

**The Torah** refers to the entire Jewish Bible and to the whole body of Jewish law and teachings. It is the body of the Scripture known to non-Jews as the Old Testament. Let us look at what Christians believe about money in comparison to what Jews believe about money.

# What Christians Believe about Money

The Christians' view about wealth is balanced with eternal values. That balance has weakened the resolve of some Christians to be wealthy. According to some Jews, the New Testament and the Christian world have an ambivalent attitude toward money and wealth. This means the Christian view on acquiring wealth is uncertain, contradictory and sometimes fluctuating. They quote such Scriptures as the ones below that show Christians to be somewhat disapproving of real wealth. This uncertain belief system about the usefulness of wealth contributes to an uncertain pattern of wealth distribution among Christians.

*"Easier for a camel to pass through the eye of a needle than for someone who is rich to enter the kingdom of God"* (Matthew 19:24, Luke 18:25, Mark 10:25).

*"You cannot serve God and wealth"* (Luke 16:13).

*"If we have food and clothing, we will content with these. But those who want to be rich fall in to temptation and are trapped by many senseless and harmful desires that plunge people on to ruin and destruction"* (1 Timothy 6:8-9).

*"For the love of money is the root of all kinds of evil."* (1 Timothy 6:10)[5]

# What Jews Believe about Money

But for the Jews, wealth is a good thing, a worthy and respectable goal to strive toward. What's more, once you earn it, it is tragic to lose it. Judaism has never considered poverty a virtue. The first Jews were not poor, and that was good.

The Jewish founding fathers, Abraham, Isaac and Jacob, were blessed with cattle and land in abundance. Asceticism and self-denial are not Jewish ideals. According to the Jewish belief system, with your financial house in order, it is easier to pursue your spiritual life.[5]

# What Jews Believe about Giving

**1.    The Talmud:** "You're only as wealthy as the amount you are able to give."

**2.    The Torah:** "You are forbidden to reap the whole harvest; a remnant in the corner must be left for the poor."

**3.    The Degrees of Tzedakah:**

Jews and non-Jews differ on their views of charitable giving. Jews are taught that charity is an obligation rooted in social justice, not in love or pity for their fellow man. The word for charity in Hebrew is tzedakah, from the root word zedek meaning "justice" or "righteousness". Moses Maimonides, a twelfth century scholar and philosopher, determined that there are eight degrees of tzedakah. Jews therefore have eight levels or stages of giving:

Stage 1:    The person gives reluctantly.

Stage 2:    The person gives graciously, but less than his or her means.

Stage 3:    The person gives the proper amount, but only after being asked.

Stage 4:    The person gives before being asked.

Stage 5:    The person gives without knowledge of the recipient, but the recipient knows the donor.

Stage 6:     The person gives without making his or her own identity known.

Stage 7:     The person gives without knowing the recipient and without making his or her identity known.

Stage 8:     The person helps another by enabling that person to become self-sufficient through a gift or loan, or helping him gain or find employment.[6]

# Do the Jews Actually Practise These Things?

In spite of the stereotype that they are miserly, Jews are the most philanthropic group of people in America. Their ability to organize and utilize economic power has been a prime source of the Jewish-American community's strength. Their charitable giving not only supports their expanded world community; it also helps individual Jews up the economic ladder.[7]

A list of facts about Jewish-American giving reveals a wealthy, generous and liberally active community.

## Six Facts about Jewish Giving

1.     The average American gives 2 percent of disposable income to charity, compared to 4 percent for the average Jew.

2.     The annual campaign for the United Jewish Appeal (UJA) collects about $1billion annually, drawing from 2 percent of the total population. The United Way annual campaign, in contrast, attracts 32 million contributors and raises $ 3.6 billion.[8]

3.     With the possible exception of the Salvation Army, the United Jewish Appeal raises more money than any other individual charity in America, including the American Red Cross, Catholic Charities and the American Cancer Society.[9]

4.     Total Jewish philanthropic giving totalled about $4.5 billion in 1997. This includes $1.5 billion to federations including UJA, $2 billion to synagogues, $700 million sent to Israel outside UJA (which came to be known as United Jewish Communities in 1999), and $250 million for educational, religious and community relations, institutions and agencies.[10]

97

5.     Among the nation's most generous donors, Jews are prominent. Worth magazine's annual "Benefactor 100" contained thirty-five Jewish philanthropists in April 1999.[11]

6.     The impressive amount of Jewish philanthropy is due not only to Jewish wealth but also to well-organized and massive efforts to raise funds for Jewish causes.  It serves as a model for other groups that want to create an effective fund-raising organization to meet monetary goals year after year.[12]

*Chapter 13*

# A Modern Rabbi
# Teaches on Prosperity

Over hundreds of years, the connection between giving charity and increased wealth has been observed. Ancient Jewish wisdom is not describing a behaviour as much as it is describing a reality. Giving money away increases the wealth of the donor. Many Jews are still raised today knowing that giving charity is not only a good thing to do but is also a rather smart thing for the richest people to do. If you seek out philanthropic friends, you too will hear accounts that appear to mysteriously link effect to cause; the effect of wealth caused by giving charity.

All religious traditions stress the importance of giving to charity; however, Judaism's impact on its followers is augmented by its unique approach to charity. The *Midrash* on the Book of Proverbs for instance insists that, **"If you see someone donating to charity, be assured that his wealth is increasing"**.

The almost impenetrable textbook of Jewish mysticism, the esoteric *Zohar*, states, **"He who donates much to charity becomes richer because of it inasmuch as he opens up a channel for God's blessing to reach him."** What is the value of these ancient statements of faith to a modern, and perhaps even secularized, business professional? Just this: They have survived as part of a living culture of oral transmission. That means something. It means they have passed the test of credibility.

# JEWISH TRADITIONAL BELIEFS ON WEALTH CREATION THROUGH GIVING

## 1. JEWS BELIEVE THAT: Charitable giving benefits the giver.

JEWISH TRADITION TEACHES ITS ADHERENTS THAT MANY OF ITS REQUIRED ACTIONS ARE FOR REFLECTIVE REASONS. FOR INSTANCE, THE BIBLE IS EMPHATIC ABOUT PROHIBITING CRUELTY TO ANIMALS. Urging kindness to animals is not because Judaism views animals as independent beings with rights not to be molested or subjected to any cruel treatment. Instead, Judaism warns that inflicting cruelty on animals brings about a coarsening of the human personality. You must be kind to animals because doing so turns you into a more sensitive and more vital person.

Jews are even instructed in how they ought to behave toward certain inanimate objects. Again, this is not because the inanimate object cares about how it is created. It is because someone who is careful about how she interacts with even inanimate objects is someone who will become supersensitive about how she interacts with people.

Finally, there is the example in which the Bible prohibits cursing a deaf man. Although the disabled victim does not hear the invective being hurled in his direction, it is still forbidden behaviour because cursing anyone does more harm to the curser than to the recipient.

In similar fashion, Jews give money away regardless of how much the government is doing to solve a problem. They give money away regardless of whether they actually would be doing more social good by investing those funds in a profit-seeking venture capital fund. They also give money away regardless of the fact that sometimes people who actually make use of the supported facilities could easily foot the bill. THEY GIVE MONEY AWAY BECAUSE ON SOME DEEP LEVEL, THEY RECOGNIZE THAT DOING SO DOES MORE FOR THE GIVER THAN IT DOES FOR THE RECIPIENT.

Jews do not give money away because it is always rational to do so, but in spite of the fact that it is often irrational.

Jews give money away not because it is rational but because it is right.

ONE OF THE MOST IMPORTANT HABITS THAT ANYONE INTERESTED IN INCREASING WEALTH SHOULD ACQUIRE IS GIVING AWAY MONEY. This appears to be paradoxical. Accumulating money would appear to be easier if you held on to every dollar you receive rather than following this irrational advice. Yet, it is good advice. IT MAY BE IRRATIONAL AND IT MAY EVEN BE COUNTER-INTUITIVE, BUT IT IS GOOD ADVICE.[13]

2. **JEWS BELIEVE THAT:** You must not live beyond your means; instead give beyond your means. Giving money away makes more come back to you.

People are suspicious of doing business with desperate people. Desperate people make others uncomfortable. Apart from anything else, their pathetic eagerness makes others doubt the value of the prospective purchase. People are also uneasy about others who appear overeager to become friendly. Premature use of first names or other very informal salutations, like using someone's nickname before having been invited to do so, can have the same effect.

One of the very best ways of overcoming that appearance of desperate eagerness is to make yourself feel rich. If you were rich, then another deal would be nice but not crucial. That is exactly the perception the other party should have of you. That way she will say to herself, "What can he do for me?" However, if you come across as needy and desperate, she is saying to herself, "I wonder what he wants from me?"

This is why one of the most used sales techniques is to suggest an urgency. For instance, "This sale ends at midnight tonight!" or "This is the very last suit in this color that I have left." That immediately turns the tables. Now it is no longer a desperate salesperson pushing a product, it is more a case of an increasingly desperate customer – you – hoping the kind, helpful salesperson will get you the product you want. You have suddenly been transformed into a very compliant customer.

That salesperson was transformed into a bigger person, somebody who could do something for you rather than someone who wanted to separate you from your money.

SIMILARLY, IF YOU HAD SOME MAGICAL METHOD OF TURNING YOURSELF INTO A LARGER, NON-DESPERATE KIND OF PERSON, SOMEONE WHO WAS SEEN TO BE MORE OF A GIVER THAN A TAKER, YOUR BUSINESS INTERACTIONS WOULD DRAMATICALLY IMPROVE. If you somehow genuinely felt yourself to be a bigger person than you might really be, the perception of you would change until you had effectively made yourself bigger.

ONE OF THE POPULAR WAYS TO ACCOMPLISH THIS IS BY SPENDING MONEY.[14]

## 3. JEWS BELIEVE THAT: You must give money, not just to do good but to do well.

Jewish tradition asks how the cowardly spies could possibly have known how they appeared in the eyes of the local inhabitants? Nobody really knows how others view him or her. The answer serves as a valuable warning for all time. If you feel like a grasshopper, then you will most certainly appear to be one from the perspective of those around you. If you feel desperate and then consequently perhaps a little self-focused, then that is exactly how you will appear in the eyes of those around you. Too bad people don't really like doing business, or having any other close contact, with individuals who radiate selfishness. If you don't want to come across to others as a grasshopper, take care not to feel like one. This is easier said than done. HOW CAN YOU AVOID FEELING A BIT LIKE A GRASSHOPPER WHEN YOU ARE FEELING HEAVY PRESSURES? AVOID IT BY GIVING MONEY AWAY.[15]

## 4.     JEWS BELIEVE THAT:  Being charitable means making new friends.

It is tough to give money away without becoming INVOLVED WITH MANY OTHER PEOPLE.

## 5.     JEWS BELIEVE THAT:     Donating is like investing; it increases what comes back to you.

Charitable giving is a powerful tool to use in increasing your own income because it helps you train yourself to become an EFFECTIVE INVESTOR.  If you have the generosity of spirit to give money away, you also have the courage to seek profit by placing your money at risk.[16]

## 6.     JEWS BELIEVE THAT:  People are creators not consumers, and givers not takers.

Naturally, once you think of someone in a certain way, you act in accordance with your thoughts. That is why you do not act identically toward all strangers.  When encountering a stranger, your mind picks up clues from clothing, conduct, context and occupation and draws a conclusion; and you act accordingly in your style of greeting and in how you interact with that person.

HUMANS ARE NOT TAKERS BY NATURE. HUMANS DO FAR BETTER AS GIVERS.   THEY LIKE TO SEE THEMSELVES AS GIVERS, AND THEY TEND TO BE GRACIOUS AS GIVERS, RATHER THAN AS TAKERS.

Giving charity is another way of ensuring that you always see yourself as a giver, rather than as a taker; your drive is to achieve, your persistence, and your very zest for life are all enormously enhanced when you see yourself as a giver, rather than as a taker. MAKING THE ACT OF GIVING REGULAR CHARITABLE DONATIONS A LIFE HABIT, IS ONE WAY TO MAKE SURE THAT YOU VIEW YOURSELF AS A GIVER.[17]

# THREE JEWISH PRINCIPLES THAT LEAD TO THE PATH OF PROSPERITY

### 1. Don't try to find a rational reason for giving away money:

Charity is irrational. Nevertheless, it benefits the giver in many ways. You give money away not because it is rational but because it is right. It is part of the traditional way of life in the United States.

### 2. Give money away because it is one of the most powerful and effective ways of increasing your own income:

More than just a few business lunches are scheduled as a result of chance encounters during charitable support work. Rest assured that in very little time, you will be involved in transactions, partnerships, or collaborations that grew from your association with your charitable group.

### 3. Keep in mind that giving away money is like investing:

In the case of charity, you give away money with the idea that it may one day come back to you in plentiful returns, but perhaps it may not. There are no guarantees. The same is true of investing money and effort in your own enterprise. Your investment may one day produce great returns. However, it is just possible that nothing will come of it. But you should do it anyway. Giving away money keeps your investment muscle fully exercised and ready for opportunity.[18]

## JEWISH TESTIMONY

### "Giving Away 10 Percent of Your After-Tax Income"

Hanna Bandes worked as a professional storyteller, using her dramatic skills to excite both children and adults about Jewish history and traditions. To drum up business, she developed a mailing list of synagogues and religious schools to which she sent regular advertising mailings. Her very first paid job was for a local synagogue. She describes it as having been such an embarrassing disaster that she removed that institution's address from her future mailings, knowing that it would never hire her again. Hanna said, "The life of an artist can be precarious, and besides telling stories I did temporary work to make ends meet. Every month I paid my bills, but sometimes it was a real struggle. I knew of the Torah rule about tithing from my earnings, but in my financial position I didn't see how I could possibly give ten percent. I rationalized that since I was performing for Jewish charitable organizations, I was giving time instead of money."

Then one evening, she found herself inspired by a speaker who explained the value of tithing from one's income. On the spot, she decided she would donate to charity 10 percent of the fees from her very next storytelling job which is exactly what she did. A few days later, Hanna received a phone call from the synagogue where she had given that first miserable performance. "We've built a new sanctuary and will be dedicating it. Will you tell stories at our dedication? I'm afraid all we can offer is $xxx," the lady on the phone told Hanna, mentioning a fee far higher than she would have asked.

A coincidence, perhaps, but Hanna believes not. "That wasn't the only job that came in unexpectedly. Within weeks of deciding to give away ten percent of my storytelling income, that income doubled. And the principle has proven to be true in the ensuing years. AS LONG AS I TITHE, MY FREELANCE INCOME IS RELIABLE. IF I FORGET, IT DRIES UP."[19]

*Chapter 14*

# How Tithers Fulfil the Laws of Wealth Creation

Wealth creation is not as straightforward as it may seem. There are many studies that look into how rich countries became rich and why poor countries stay poor. The poverty of the peoples of the world and its causes have been studied and analysed by many different people. Human beings have tried many times to pinpoint the causes of the inequalities in this world.

All these different studies have revealed certain patterns in the lives of wealthy people. Studies that analyse large numbers of people reveal new and valuable information to seekers of truth. It is interesting that the legendary wealth of Jews has been noted all over the world for centuries. This wealth has generated a lot of jealousy and persecution for Jews, culminating in the holocaust.

Wealth is mysterious! Generating wealth is even more mysterious! What you may think makes somebody wealthy is often not what has made him wealthy. One of the mystical contributions to wealth creation is actually the giving away of wealth. Giving away money should actually reduce your wealth. This is simple arithmetic. Amazingly, giving away wealth seems to create wealth. This is a reality proven by many secular and historic facts.

In this chapter, I will share with you why wealth is created by people who tithe and give away money.

## 1.   Tithing Christians fulfil the law of humility, which creates wealth.

For promotion cometh neither from the east, nor from the west, nor from the south. But God is the judge: he putteth down one, and setteth up another.

Psalm 75:6-7

It is the fool who says in his heart that there is no God. Wealth comes from God. Blessing comes from God. Except the Lord build the house they labour in vain. When a person tithes, he demonstrates his recognition of the God-factor in his very existence. He demonstrates his respect for God's input in his life. He declares his gratitude to God for helping him. A person who tithes therefore fulfils the law of humility.

Humility has been shown to be an important factor in wealth creation. Arrogant wealthy empires have crumbled through their pride. Political parties have lost their power through pride and complacency. Successful companies have been wiped out when the management lost their original humble attitudes.

Paying tithes helps you remember that you did not make it on your own. Paying tithes causes you to bow your knees to your Creator each time you receive money. Paying tithes causes you to humble yourself before a priest whom you may have otherwise despised.

Many arrogant and rich people have no time for priests or pastors. They see them as hyenas and vultures scavenging for the scraps of the successful and wealthy. When wealthy people have to pay tithes for the upkeep of these "irrelevant members of society", it will help them to stay humble.

Any business man who stays humble will generate wealth for himself. Any Christian who maintains a humble attitude will create wealth for himself. Paying tithes forces you to humbly submit to the priest and the pastor of the day for your own good.

## 2.    Tithing Christians fulfil the law of sowing and reaping, which creates wealth.

Every farmer creates wealth for himself when he sows his seeds in the right season. The oldest law of wealth creation is embodied in the principle of sowing and reaping. Ancient farmers who did not know modern economic theories at least knew that they would reap a harvest if they sowed the right seeds. The Bible is replete with Scriptures that teach on the principles of sowing and reaping.

Paying tithes activates the laws of sowing and reaping because the tithe is a seed that you sow in the house of God.

Everyone therefore who pays tithes, sows a seed and qualifies for a harvest. The Scriptures below show the blessings which result from sowing seeds. These Scriptures predict that after sowing your tithes in sorrow, you will reap in joy. They also show why the tithe will be multiplied and given back to you many times over.

They that **sow** in tears shall **reap** in joy.

Psalm 126:5

**Give, and it shall be given unto you;** good measure, pressed down, and shaken together, and running over, shall men give into your bosom. For with the same measure that ye mete withal it shall be measured to you again.

Luke 6:38

## 3.    Tithing Christians fulfil the law of prioritisation, which creates wealth.

But seek ye first the kingdom of God, and his righteousness; and all these things shall be added unto you.

Matthew 6:33

There is no prosperous person who does not fulfil the law of prioritisation. When you are young, you need to prioritise your education and put first things first. Without prioritising education, your youthful years will pass away and you will be bereft of a much-needed education. You will therefore inflict upon yourself a severe debilitating poverty that lasts a lifetime. Failing to prioritise education in your youthful life can lead to poverty.

Failing to prioritise in any sphere of life always leads to failure. If you filled your stomach with sweets first and were therefore unable to eat proper food, you would not have a balanced diet and you would not be healthy. Once again, it is all about priorities.

Companies that fail to remember their priorities always end up in disaster. Churches can likewise forget the reasons why they exist and start to emphasize secular things like success and wealth. But the priority of the church is Christ Jesus and the salvation of this world.

The ability to get your priorities right is important and will always lead to wealth.

Tithing presents an important test in prioritisation. When a person learns to pay his tithes, he learns to put God first. Tithing helps you acquire the habit of dealing with the most important thing first. This habit of prioritisation will extend to other areas and lead to success in life. This is one of the reasons why tithers become wealthy people.

## 4. Tithing Christians fulfil the law of emulation, which creates wealth.

That ye be not slothful, but followers of them who through faith and patience inherit the promises.

Hebrews 6:12

Emulation is the art of copying something others are doing. Abramovitz, the economist, spoke of surging forward and catching up with those ahead. This is emulation and is what rich nations did to become wealthy.

Simply put, rich nations became rich by copying what successful nations around them did. For instance in 1957, when the Soviet Union stepped ahead of the world with the Sputnik programme (a series of robotic spacecraft missions), America emulated the activities of Russia by setting up NASA the following year in 1958. America did not decide to specialise in farming and leave Russia to develop space technology. They decided to surge forward and catch up with the Soviet Union.

It is through such acts of emulation that most of the rich and developed world became who they are today.

Countries like Korea that shamelessly copied industrial secrets and practices of western countries have equally caught up and become rich.

Emulation is therefore a well-known strategy for developing wealth. Do what the rich people did to become rich!

Don't bother with what they *say*, just do what they *did* to become wealthy!

Copying is the most primitive and uninhibited form of learning. It is therefore nature's highest and best way of learning because it is the method created by God. Emulation or copying occurs throughout nature and leads to speedy development.

The Jews are known for their legendary wealth. They are actually hated because of their success and riches. **One of the**

110

**chief practices of Jews is tithing. Tithing, therefore is an activity of the legendarily rich.** If you want to be rich you must emulate rich people. I am sure whoever is reading this book has a desire to be successful and even rich. Why don't you emulate the Jews whose legendary wealth has brought them such fame and jealousy?

The Bible teaches about emulation in Hebrews 6:12. It teaches us to follow people who have succeeded in what they did. Famous Bible characters like Abraham and Jacob tithed.

Solomon, the richest man who ever lived, practised tithing. Is it any wonder to you if tithing is recommended as a practice that can lead to wealth? After all, the rich, successful people you wish to be like practised tithing!

## 5.    Tithing Christians understand the law of seasons, and this creates wealth.

The earth has been created to operate in seasons. There is a time to sow seeds and there is a time to reap what is sown. There is a time when it is cold and there is a time when it is hot. It is only those who have understood the concept of the seasons who truly prosper. A farmer who goes out to sow his seeds in winter is wasting his time. He will not prosper and he will not be successful. His failure is because he does not understand the season. Similarly, there are political seasons and even financial cycles. If you understand these cycles, you will operate very successfully within them.

Joseph warned Pharaoh of a coming season which would wipe out the prosperity of the day. Pharaoh listened to him and survived the coming season of lean cows. "Behold, there come seven years of great plenty throughout all the land of Egypt: and there shall arise after them seven years of famine; and all the plenty shall be forgotten in the land of Egypt; and the famine shall consume the land; and the plenty shall not be known in the land by reason of that famine following; for it shall be very grievous" (Genesis 41:29-31).

111

The practise of tithing calls for recognition of seasons. If you do not understand how life operates in seasons you will not make optimum use of the season you are in.

A person who practises tithing demonstrates that he recognizes the season for sowing seeds. He demonstrates that he will be expecting a season of harvest in the future. He shows that he is fully aware of the fact that things do not remain the same forever. Everything we have is for a season. **All enduring wealth is created by men who took advantage of the season of sowing when it came.** God is teaching you about tithing so that you will become one of the people who flows successfully with the seasons of life.

> **There is a right time for everything: a time to be born; a time to die; A TIME TO PLANT; A TIME TO HARVEST;**
>
> **Ecclesiastes 3:1-2 (TLB)**

God is giving you a season to plant the seed of the tithe. The "tithe seeds" you have sown will give you a harvest in the future. You will benefit greatly when others are struggling because you sowed the seed of the tithe.

## 6. Tithing Christians understand the law of a willing attitude, which creates wealth.

> **IF YE BE WILLING and obedient, YE SHALL EAT THE GOOD OF THE LAND: But if ye refuse and rebel, ye shall be devoured with the sword: for the mouth of the LORD hath spoken it.**
>
> **Isaiah 1:19-20**

The attitude of a person determines his altitude. As an employer, I long to work with people who have a good attitude. Your willingness and flowing attitude are more important than your real abilities. Everyone loves to work with eager positive people. Perhaps, a willing attitude has taken more people higher than anything else.

The attitude of a person is always shown when he is asked to do things he does not understand. There are many jobs and tasks that will require your willingness rather than your understanding.

Tithing calls upon that essential willing attitude! Without a positive willing attitude, you cannot give away ten percent of your hard-earned income.

Most of us need more than a hundred percent of our incomes to just survive. It does not make sense to give away ten percent of your income to vague, undefined spiritual causes. Without a willing attitude you will not practise tithing! Tithing therefore develops within you a flowing willing attitude for something you cannot fully understand. It is this same willing attitude that will take you higher in other spheres of life. There is more hope for a willing person than a stubborn unyielding personality.

## 7. Tithing Christians understand the law of obedience, which creates wealth.

The ability to obey instructions is another quality that generates wealth. Obedient people go further than disobedient ones. This is easy to see. I love people who obey my instructions. Don't you?

Many of the greatest tests of your life are simply tests of obedience.

Tithing is yet another test of obedience. It is a test that you will have to pass if you are going to do well. Obey God and give him ten percent of everything you have. Perhaps, the great harvest of the tither is the harvest of the seeds of obedience.

Dear friend, tithing is an important exercise even if it is just an exercise in blind obedience. You cannot be trusted with certain positions if you are not obedient. You cannot be trusted with certain amounts of money if you are not obedient to the one who gives it to you. The blessing is for the obedient. Jesus said, "if you love me you will obey me." You prove your love for God by your obedience.

Saul lost his right to the throne because of disobedience. Perhaps you will lose your right to certain great positions of authority because you failed to obey God in the matter of tithing. Do not let tithing be the stumbling block over which you lose your blessing and promotion. Do not be like Saul who was rejected because he disobeyed God in a simple matter.

**And Samuel said, Hath the LORD as great delight in burnt offerings and sacrifices, as in obeying the voice of the LORD? Behold, to obey is better than sacrifice, and to hearken than the fat of rams.**

**For rebellion is as the sin of witchcraft, and stubbornness is as iniquity and idolatry. Because thou hast rejected the word of the LORD, he hath also rejected thee from being king.**

**1 Samuel 15:22-23**

*Chapter 15*

# How Tithers Activate the Laws of Sowing and Reaping

The farmers of this world have long known the laws of sowing and reaping. They have consistently activated these laws for their own benefit and have learnt not to violate them. Those who understand and deploy the laws of sowing and reaping are wealthy.

In the beginning, God created the seed in living things giving them the mysterious power to reproduce themselves. Seeds are mysterious things. They have a plan and they have life hidden deep within them. They are small but are the reason for all that we see. Every animal you see today is the result of a seed. On the average, lions live for about eight years in the wild and about twenty years in the zoo. Obviously, the lions you see around have not been there since the Creation. The miracle of Creation happened a long time ago. But it is the miracle of the seed that has sustained the Creation and produced every living thing around you. It is important to understand the way seeds work because seeds contain the miracle power of growth and reproduction.

We all know about the seeds of plants and trees. But the bible teaches us about many other seeds, including our money and our gifts. Even though money is a lifeless inanimate object, it contains the mysterious power of a seed. Notice this passage in which Paul continuously refers to our gifts, contributions and money as seeds. "Now this I say, he who sows sparingly will also reap sparingly, and he who sows bountifully will also reap bountifully.

Each one must do just as he has purposed in his heart, not grudgingly or under compulsion, for God loves a cheerful giver.

"And God is able to make all grace abound to you, so that always having all sufficiency in everything, you may have an abundance for every good deed; as it is written, 'He scattered abroad, He gave to the poor, His righteousness endures forever.' Now He who supplies seed to the sower and bread for food will supply and multiply your seed for sowing and increase the harvest of your righteousness" (2 Corinthians 9:6-10, NASB).

Every time you give your tithes, you are sowing a seed into the house of God. Paying tithes activates the laws of sowing seeds and reaping harvests! Tithing Christians therefore fulfil several important laws of sowing and reaping and inadvertently create wealth for themselves. Let us now discuss the laws of sowing and reaping which are set in motion by tithing.

## The Fifteen Laws of Sowing and Reaping

### 1.    You must PLANT SOMETHING.

**Verily, verily, I say unto you, EXCEPT A CORN OF WHEAT FALL INTO THE GROUND and die, IT ABIDETH ALONE: but if it die, it bringeth forth much fruit.**

**John 12:24**

The first law of the sowing and reaping teaches that you must plant *something*. You must actually have a seed that you have sown. If you have not sown anything you cannot expect anything. The less spiritual you are, the less you will correlate things that happen to you with seeds you have planted in the past. The more spiritual you are, the more you will expect a harvest of seeds you have planted.

One day, I was on the golf course with some friends. A friend of mine was teeing off and someone standing by began to mock and laugh at him. My friend felt embarrassed and was barely able to hit his ball. We continued to play and walked down the golf course to the next hole. I noticed that my friend had become quiet. As we walked along, he suddenly left us and walked towards another group that was playing on another hole. I realized that he was walking towards the person that had jeered at him. We continued playing and soon enough he joined us again.

I asked him, "What happened? Did you go to talk to those people?"

"Yes," he answered. "I went to sort them out."

"What did you tell them," I asked.

He answered, "I told him we were all gentlemen on the course and I did not expect to be mocked at in public. Everybody has a time that he learns how to play! I don't need to come to the golf course to be mocked at."

"Wow," I said. "That's powerful. How did they feel?"

He said, "I don't know but he had no right to mock at me in that way."

Then he made a remarkable statement.

He said, *"I have not sown that seed to reap it. I have not sown such seeds."*

What he meant was that he had not planted such seeds of public mockery and he did not expect to reap the experience of being mocked at in public.

You see, my friend was a spiritual person and he saw things in the light of sowing and reaping. He did not see why he should experience a harvest of public ridicule when he had not ridiculed others in the past.

You must begin to see things in the light of sowing and reaping. Every farmer does. Whether you like it or not many things you deal with are actually results of seeds you have sown. Many things you do are actually seeds that you are sowing. You can expect a harvest when you have planted a seed. Paying your tithes is the planting of a seed. Paying your tithes opens the door for you to reap financially in the future.

## 2.　You must PLANT IN GOOD GROUND.

**But other fell into GOOD GROUND, and brought forth fruit, some an hundredfold, some sixtyfold, some thirtyfold.**

**Matthew 13:8**

The second important law of sowing and reaping is that you must plant in good ground. Seeds do not grow everywhere. Apple trees do not grow in tropical Africa. Their seeds simply do not flourish in the dry red West African soil. However, they are able to flourish in temperate climates.

Your seed will flourish when you plant it into a good church. If you plant your seed into a dead ministry that has departed from the Scriptures, do not expect any harvest.

## 3.　You must plant LARGE AMOUNTS OF SEED!

Another important principle of seed sowing is the fact that *large amounts of seed must be sown.* Large amounts of seed are needed because many seeds are lost in the process of being planted. Very few seeds end up in the right place. Because of this fact, large amounts of seed must be sown. Every business makes its projections with this in mind. Most businesses calculate their profits, expecting to suffer losses, stealing, accidents and unfortunate events. Large amounts of seed must always be sown because of the inevitable losses.

**But remember this-if you give little, you will get little. A farmer who plants just a few seeds WILL GET ONLY A SMALL CROP, but if he plants much, HE WILL REAP MUCH**

**2 Corinthians 9:6 (TLB)**

## 4. Some of your SEEDS WILL BE LOST.

Another important truth about sowing seeds is that many of them will be lost. The reason why a man has millions of sperms is because most of them are simply lost on the way to the good ground. I was shocked to find that when a man has less than forty million sperms he will have difficulty in achieving a pregnancy.

This truth means that some of the offerings you give will be lost as seed that falls by the wayside. There is no way to determine which one will be lost and which one will fall onto good ground. That is why you just have to keep on sowing because some of your seeds will be lost anyway. Coming to church many times and being given many opportunities to give your tithes and offerings will definitely increase your chances of reaping a harvest.

**Hearken; Behold, there went out a sower to sow:**

**And it came to pass, as he sowed, SOME FELL BY THE WAY SIDE, and the fowls of the air came and devoured it up.**

**And SOME FELL ON STONY GROUND, where it had not much earth; and immediately it sprang up, because it had no depth of earth:**

**Mark 4:3-5**

## 5.    Some of your SEEDS WILL NEVER DEVELOP.

**And some fell among thorns; and the THORNS sprung up, and choked them:**

**Matthew 13:7**

Another reality about seeds is the fact that some of the seeds will never develop.

A farmer once told me of how he spent his savings to purchase some day-old chicks for his chicken farm. These day-old chicks were the seeds of investment for his chicken farm. But the farmer had a sad story to tell.

He told me, "After I purchased these day-old chicks I fed them earnestly and waited for them to grow, but they simply didn't grow."

He told me, "I tried everything I could. I got the vet to come. I gave them extra food. I gave them vitamins. I spent so much money on these chickens but they simply did not grow!"

What this poor farmer did not know was that there was something inherently wrong with the chicks. He had purchased chicks that did not have the ability to grow.

I found out from a more experienced chicken farmer that this was a problem with many day-old chicks. Some of the stock simply did not grow no matter what was done for them. There are seeds like that. They simply lack the ability to develop.

I once planted a mango tree in my house. After eight years, I was still taller than the mango tree. I decided that there was no point in keeping that mango tree because there was something essentially wrong with it. I had planted the wrong seed and it simply was not working.

These are the reasons why farmers do not plant only a single seed. They know too well that many seeds will not grow.

But there is good news. The one seed which does grow will be worth all the ones that did not grow. The few seeds that land on good ground will be worth all the wasted millions of seeds that you have sown.

## 6.    You must plant the TYPE OF SEEDS you expect.

If you want coconuts you must plant a coconut. If you want mango fruits you must plant mangoes. If you want money you must plant money. You can only expect a fruit that corresponds with what you have sown.

**And the earth brought forth grass, and HERB YIELDING SEED AFTER HIS KIND, and the tree yielding fruit, whose seed was in itself, after his kind: and God saw that it was good.**

**Genesis 1:12**

## 7.    Your SEED MUST DIE.

Every seed must die. It undergoes decomposition and virtually melts away. This is what happens when you plant your seed in the house of God. It enters the offering basket and melts away. You are forced to forget about it. You can no longer identify it as a traceable object. It has disappeared. It belongs to the church and it's all mixed up with everything else. Some people want to follow their money and watch its every movement. But you must allow it to melt away and disappear.

**Verily, verily, I say unto you, except a corn of wheat fall into the ground and DIE, it abideth alone: but if it die, it bringeth forth much fruit.**

**John 12:24**

## 8.    Your seed must be given TIME TO DIE.

Your seed also needs time to die. A watched pot never boils. If you keep watching the seed, it will seem to you that it never dies and never germinates. You must forget about it and decide never to remember the seed you have sown. When you do that,

121

you would have given your seed enough time to go through the processes it must go through.

**Cast thy bread upon the waters: for thou shalt find it after many days.**

**Ecclesiastes 11:1**

## 9. Your seed will grow by GOD'S MIRACLE POWER.

**I have planted, Apollos watered; but GOD GAVE THE INCREASE.**

**1 Corinthians 3:6**

**And he said, So is the kingdom of God, as if a man should cast seed into the ground; and should sleep, and rise night and day, and the seed should spring and grow up, HE KNOWETH NOT HOW.**

**Mark 4:26-27**

No one really knows how a seed grows into a mighty tree. Scientists have tried to analyse what exactly happens to the seed. Ultimately, it is a miracle that a seed can grow into a mighty tree. Think about it; somebody as big as you, who has a heart, kidney, stomach and brains grew out of an invisible seed. It is all a miracle.

We often ask ourselves the question, "How will my five dollar seed turn into thousands of dollars." It is impossible, says the natural mind. But through the miracle power of God, your five dollar seed can actually become a million dollars. Don't ask me why because I do not know. I just accept it as a fact of faith. I know it happens. I believe it happens because I am a believer.

If you believe in this reality, you will be happy to pay your tithes. You will know that it is not a waste of ten percent of your income. You will know that it is the investment of a seed into the good ground of a church. You will know that it is the investment of a seed into the miracle power of God.

## 10.  You must RECOGNIZE YOUR HARVEST when it comes.

There are people who are good givers but poor receivers. To successfully activate the laws of sowing and reaping, you must be a *good giver* as well as a *good receiver.* To receive, you must recognize the day of the harvest. You must see when God is blessing you and you must recognize the different ways in which He allows you to reap the seeds you have sown. If you were to count your blessings, perhaps you would see how good the Lord has been to you.

Many times, the Lord returns your harvest in a way you never expected. Ask God to open your eyes so that you appreciate His blessings and the harvest of your seeds.

**For the kingdom of heaven is like unto a man that is an householder, which went out early in the morning to HIRE LABOURERS into his vineyard.**

**Matthew 20:1**

## 11.  You must become a HUMBLE RECEIVER.

It takes humility to receive gifts from people. Many givers are too proud to receive gifts from others. They say to themselves, "I don't want anyone to think that I need anything. I don't want anyone to think that I lack something."

It is that pride which keeps people away from the priesthood. People are kept away from the priesthood because pastors need humility to receive gifts from people. Without humility you cannot receive. Pride cries out from within, "I have need of no one. I need nothing. I am independent."

Be careful, because we all need one another.

## 12.  Do not refrain from sowing UNLIKELY SEEDS.

There are many seeds that look unlikely to prosper. One day, I held the hand of a brother who was sowing a seed of five dollars. I said to him, "This is a car." The next day someone called him and gave him a car. How could that be? It was an unlikely five dollar seed but it turned out to be a great blessing. This is why the Bible says, "In the morning sow thy seed, and in the evening withhold not thine hand: for thou knowest not whether shall prosper, either this or that, or whether they both shall be alike good" (Ecclesiastes 11:6).

For many years, the economy of Ghana has depended on cocoa. A cocoa seed was brought to Ghana by a gentleman called Tetteh-Quarshie. He carried this seed in his bag from Fernando Po. What an unlikely seed! But that seed carried the future economy of an entire nation. In Tetteh-Quarshie's bag were all the buildings of the nation Ghana; all its military equipment of its future army, the salaries of all the government workers and the future industries of the country. What a miracle he was carrying in his bag and what an unlikely seed!

This is why you must never withhold your hand when it is time to give an offering or pay your tithes. Perhaps the tithes you pay in June will become a seed to pay your children's school fees in future. Perhaps the tithes you pay this month will be the seeds for your personal home.

## 13.    USE SOME of your harvest AS A SEED.

**For God, who gives seed to the farmer TO PLANT, and later on good crops to harvest and eat, will give you more and more SEED TO PLANT and will make it grow so that you can give away more and more fruit from your harvest.**

**2 Corinthians 9:10 (TLB)**

When the blessings come, remember to pay your tithes and honour God. Honouring God is the first thing you must do when you are blessed. Unfortunately, people forget the Lord in the day of their blessing. They begin to say things like, "I earn too much to pay tithes. Ten percent is too much for the church."

If you do not use part of your harvest as a seed, poverty will come upon you in the future. Do not set your eyes on money and feel secure. "...for riches certainly make themselves wings; they fly away as an eagle toward heaven" (Proverbs 23:5).

Money is deceptive. The Bible calls it the deceitfulness of riches. Money deceives! It tells you: "you will be rich forever!"

But that is not true. You need to put your trust in God. Don't let your harvest lead you to the common delusions of rich people.

## 14.    You must SAVE SOME of your harvest.

**Now therefore let Pharaoh look out a man discreet and wise, and set him over the land of Egypt.**

**Let Pharaoh do this, and let him appoint officers over the land, and take up the fifth part of the land of Egypt in the seven plenteous years.**

**And let them gather all the food of those good years that come, and lay up corn under the hand of Pharaoh, and let them keep food in the cities.**

**And that food shall be for store to the land against the seven years of famine, which shall be in the land of Egypt; that the land perish not through the famine.**

**Genesis 41:33-36**

You must also learn to save some of the harvest and blessings that God brings to you. Life is in seasons. A good season is often followed by a bad season. Different seasons are not the result of a curse somewhere. God has determined that the earth will have different seasons. "While the earth remains, Seedtime and harvest, and cold and heat, And summer and winter, And day and night Shall not cease." (Genesis 8:22, NASB).

Expect the seasons to come and go. Joseph advised Pharaoh to keep a fifth of his harvest. If you are to truly benefit from the harvest God has given you, you will need to keep part of it as savings for the season of lean cows. You will need to build houses. You will need to invest. You will need to live in such a way as to expect a season of lean cows. Because people fail to use their harvest in this way, it seems as though they never had a harvest.

Dear friend, the season of lean cows is so severe that it will eat up the season of fat cows in such a way that you will not remember that you were once blessed with a mighty harvest. "Behold, there come seven years of great plenty throughout all the land of Egypt: And there shall arise after them seven years of famine; and all THE PLENTY SHALL BE FORGOTTEN in the land of Egypt; and the famine shall consume the land; and THE PLENTY SHALL NOT BE KNOWN in the land by reason of that famine following; for it shall be very grievous (Genesis 41:29-31).

I have seen people reap blessed harvests from the Lord and end up borrowing money. It is so sad to watch people go down because they refused to follow the principle of saving some of their harvest.

## 15.    You must ENJOY SOME your harvest.

Finally, you must enjoy the harvest that God gives you. It looks as though we have the problem of either one extreme or the other. Some people are unable to enjoy the blessings that God gives. It is an evil disease to work hard and sow seeds but be unable to enjoy the fruit of your labour. Make sure you do not have this evil disease spoken of in the book of Ecclesiastes.

**A man to whom God hath given riches, wealth, and honour, so that he wanteth nothing for his soul of all that he desireth, yet God giveth him not power to eat thereof, but a stranger eateth it: this is vanity, and it is an evil disease.**

**Ecclesiastes 6:2**

*Chapter 16*

# How Tithers Make God Build a House for Them

## 1. Tithing makes provision for the house of God.

The prophet Malachi asked for the tithes to be brought to the house of the Lord for one reason: that there may be meat (supplies, provision, materials, goods, food, equipment) in the house of the Lord. The house of the Lord needs to be built. The house of the Lord also has needs. Every time you pay your tithes and offerings, you make provision for the house of the Lord.

Bring ye all the tithes into the storehouse, that there may be MEAT IN MINE HOUSE, and prove me now herewith, saith the LORD of hosts, if I will not open you the windows of heaven, and pour you out a blessing, that there shall not be room enough to receive it.

Malachi 3:10

## 2. Paying tithes is your way of investing in the house of God.

Tithing is your great seed of investment into the house of

127

God. Through your tithes you make your biggest investment into the affairs of the house of the Lord. Your tithe meets the great needs of the house of God. One of the greatest needs is for the house of God to be built, furnished and maintained.

Is it not marvellous that we can contribute to such a great and spiritual project? What is more amazing is the fact that building the house of the Lord activates the laws of sowing and reaping in a special way.

**By investing in the house of the Lord, we open ourselves to reaping a harvest of God investing in our own houses.** Tithers inadvertently invoke the blessings of God building a house for them because they build the house of God by tithing.

You will notice from the Scriptures that paying of tithes was the greatest way to invest in the house of the Lord. *Not investing* in the house of the Lord was the same as *forsaking* the house of the Lord. If God forsakes your house what will happen to you?

If you do not forsake *God's* house God will not forsake *your* house.

And we cast the lots among the priests, the Levites, and the people, for the wood offering, to bring it into the house of our God, after the houses of our fathers, at times appointed year by year, to burn upon the altar of the LORD our God, as it is written in the law:

And to BRING THE FIRSTFRUITS OF OUR GROUND, and THE FIRSTFRUITS OF ALL FRUIT OF ALL TREES, year by year, unto the house of the LORD:

Also the FIRSTBORN OF OUR SONS, AND OF OUR CATTLE, as it is written in the law, and the FIRSTLINGS OF OUR HERDS AND OF OUR FLOCKS, to bring to the house of our God, unto the priests that minister in the house of our God:

And that we should bring THE FIRSTFRUITS OF OUR DOUGH, AND OUR OFFERINGS, and the fruit of all manner of trees, of wine and of oil, unto the priests, to the chambers of the house of our God; and the tithes of our ground unto the Levites, that the same Levites might have the tithes in all the cities of our tillage.

And the priest the son of Aaron shall be with the Levites, when the Levites take tithes: and the Levites shall bring up the tithe of the tithes unto the house of our God, to the chambers, into the treasure house.

For the children of Israel and the children of Levi shall bring the offering of the corn, of the new wine, and the oil, unto the chambers, where are the vessels of the sanctuary, and the priests that minister, and the porters, and the singers: AND WE WILL NOT FORSAKE THE HOUSE OF OUR GOD.

Nehemiah 10:34-39

And I perceived that the portions of the Levites had not been given them: for the Levites and the singers, that did the work, were fled every one to his field.

Then contended I with the rulers, and said, WHY IS THE HOUSE OF GOD FORSAKEN? And I gathered them together, and set them in their place.

THEN BROUGHT ALL JUDAH THE TITHE of the corn and the new wine and the oil unto the treasuries.

And I made treasurers over the treasuries, Shelemiah the priest, and Zadok the scribe, and of the Levites, Pedaiah: and next to them was Hanan the son of Zaccur, the son of

Mattaniah: for they were counted faithful, and their office was to distribute unto their brethren.

Remember me, O my God, concerning this, and wipe not out my good deeds that I have done for the house of my God, and for the offices thereof.

Nehemiah 13:10-14

3. **You reap whatever you sow.** Many years ago, I attended the sod-cutting ceremony of a great church in our city. A great man of God performed the ceremony and made a statement which stayed with me. He said, "If you build a house for God, God will build a house for you." As I pondered on this statement, I realized that he was rephrasing Galatians six verse seven.

... for whatsoever a man soweth, that shall he also reap.

Galatians 6:7

If you invest in the house of the Lord, the Lord will invest in your house. If you plant a seed to build God's house, God will build a house for you. This is why people who pay tithes open for themselves a door to owning property.

4. **Unless God helps you, you will never own or build a house.** In many African countries, about eighty percent of urban residents live in squatter settlements or shanty towns.

Very few people in this world are able to build or own their own homes. Many people are even unable to rent houses and just use properties which they have access to. A lot of people are simply perpetual squatters.

These are facts of life. It takes the grace of God to ever have something you can call your own. That is why I declare boldly that unless God helps you, you will never own or build a house in your lifetime.

Tithing gives you an opportunity to involve God in your situation. By investing in the house of the Lord, you have sown the seeds of a house and can expect to reap a good harvest from the Lord.

Except the Lord build the house, they labour in vain that build it: except the Lord keep the city, the watchman waketh but in vain.

Psalm 127:1

5. **God objects to people living happily in their own houses when they have not made provision for the house of God.** God will oppose you living comfortably in your house when you have not built His house.

Thus speaketh the LORD of hosts, saying, this people say, The time is not come, the time that the LORD'S house should be built. Then came the word of the LORD by Haggai the prophet, saying, Is it time for you, O ye, to dwell in your cieled houses, and this house lie waste? Now therefore thus saith the LORD of hosts; Consider your ways.

Haggai 1:2-5

6. **God will be touched by your efforts to build a house for Him.** David desired to build a house for the Lord. David touched God's heart by his desire and interest in the house of the Lord. King David's attempt to build a house for the Lord invoked an amazing blessing. Notice how the Scripture puts it. God said to David in response to his attempt to invest in the house of God, "... THINE HOUSE AND THY KINGDOM SHALL BE ESTABLISHED for ever before thee: thy throne shall be established for ever (2 Samuel 7:16).

And it came to pass that night, that the word of the Lord came unto Nathan, saying, go and tell my servant David, Thus saith the Lord, Shalt thou build me an house for me to dwell in?

Whereas I have not dwelt in any house since the time that I brought up the children of Israel out of Egypt, even to this day, but have walked in a tent and in a tabernacle.

In all the places wherein I have walked with all the children of Israel spake I a word with any of the tribes of Israel, whom I commanded to feed my people Israel, saying, Why build ye not me an house of cedar?

Now therefore so shalt thou say unto my servant David, Thus saith the LORD of hosts, I took thee from the sheepcote, from following the sheep, to be ruler over my people, over Israel: and I was with thee whithersoever thou wentest, and have cut off all thine enemies out of thy sight, and have made thee a great name, like unto the name of the great men that are in the earth.

Moreover I will appoint a place for my people Israel, and will plant them, that they may dwell in a place of their own, and move no more; neither shall the children of wickedness afflict them any more, as beforetime,

And as since the time that I commanded judges to be over my people Israel, and have caused thee to rest from all thine enemies. Also the Lord telleth thee that he will make thee an house.

And when thy days be fulfilled, and thou shalt sleep with thy fathers, I will set up thy seed after thee, which shall proceed out of thy bowels, and I will establish his kingdom.

He shall build an house for my name, and I will stablish the throne of his kingdom for ever.

I will be his father, and he shall be my son. If he commit iniquity, I will chasten him with the rod of men, and with the stripes of the children of men: but my mercy shall not depart away from him, as I took it from Saul, whom I put away before thee.

And THINE HOUSE AND THY KINGDOM SHALL BE ESTABLISHED FOR EVER before thee: thy throne shall be established for ever.

2 Samuel 7:4-16

7. **God will build a house for you as He did for Solomon.** Solomon is famous for building the temple of the Lord. A little known fact is that Solomon was helped to build a mighty house for himself. Indeed, you cannot outdo God. He will bless you and build a house for you. What God did for Solomon is what He wants to do for you. Decide today to be a tither! You are deciding to build a house for God and therefore God will help you build a house for yourself.

And it came to pass in the four hundred and eightieth year after the children of Israel were come out of the land of Egypt, in the fourth year of Solomon's reign over Israel, in the month Zif, which is the second month, that HE BEGAN TO BUILD THE HOUSE OF THE LORD... In the fourth year was the foundation of the house of the Lord laid, in the month Zif: and in the eleventh year, in the month Bul, which is the eighth month, was the house finished throughout all the parts thereof, and according to all the fashion of it. So was he seven years in building it.

BUT SOLOMON WAS BUILDING HIS OWN HOUSE THIRTEEN YEARS, and he finished all his house.

1 Kings 6:1, 37-38

# Chapter 17

# How Tithers Provoke God's Graciousness

**God be gracious to us and bless us, and cause His face to shine upon us; Selah.**

**That Your way may be known on the earth, Your salvation among all nations.**

**Psalm 67:1-2**

When someone is gracious to you he shows you kindness because he loves you. A gracious person is kind, benevolent, generous, compassionate, lenient, understanding and merciful.

God's graciousness to us is revealed when He supplies our needs and gives us the abundance of all things. When we have no lack and no needs, God is being gracious to us! The houses, cars, finances that God has bestowed on us are all signs of God's graciousness!

Why is God so gracious to us? So that we can be a blessing to the nations of the world. God's graciousness is shown to us for

1) Kind
2) benevolent
3) Generous
4) Lenient
5) understands
6) Merciful
7) Compassionate

a purpose – that we may spread His Gospel to the nations. The prayer for graciousness from God is based on our promise that we would use this graciousness to spread the Gospel to the nations.

Every time you pay your tithes, you invest in God's purpose – the salvation of the nations. Paying of your tithes gives God more reasons to continue to be gracious to you.

## 1.    Tithing makes provision for the house of God.

The prophet Malachi asked for the tithes to be brought to the house of the Lord for one reason: that there may be meat (supplies, provision, materials, goods, food, equipment) in the house of the Lord. The house of the Lord exists for a purpose and every time you pay your tithes you finance that purpose.

## 2.    The House of the Lord exists to spread the word of salvation to the ends of the world.

The purpose of the house of the Lord is summarized in a statement by Jesus Christ. He said, "For the Son of man is come to seek and to save that which was lost" (Luke 19:10). This is the whole purpose of Christ's coming to the world.

## 3.    God wants to spread the news of salvation to different parts of the world and He has promised to be gracious to His people if we will help fulfil this vision.

To be gracious to someone is to show charm, kindness and a warm generosity of spirit. God will show you kindness and generosity when you help to fulfil His vision. Graciousness speaks of the kindness and warm courtesy shown by a king to his subjects. God will extend warm courtesies to you as you take up His greatest task. Indeed a person who is gracious is disposed to bestow favours and God will bestow many favours on you when you help to spread the Gospel of salvation.

4. **God's graciousness is bestowed on His church so that we would make His salvation known to the ends of the world.** Your wealth exists because of God's graciousness and blessings. If God is not gracious to you, you would not have or own anything.

God be gracious to us and bless us, and cause His face to shine upon us -- Selah.

That Your way may be known on the earth, Your salvation among all nations.

Psalm 67:1-2

5. **Your continued tithing gives God a good reason to continue to be gracious to you and bless you.**

The tithe is used to spread the Gospel and therefore God is forced to be gracious to tithers. "God be gracious to us and bless us, and cause His face to shine upon us. That Your way may be known on the earth, Your salvation among all nations" Psalm 67:1-2 (NASB).

6. **It is tithing (giving ten percent of your blessings) that enables the house of God to *send* people to preach the Gospel of salvation.**

The Gospel of salvation is spread by people who are sent all over the world as evangelists and missionaries. This costs a lot of money and the only way people are sent is if the house of the Lord has enough supplies (meat).

For whosoever shall call upon the name of the Lord shall be saved.

How then shall they call on him in whom they have not believed? and how shall they believe in him of whom they have not heard? and how shall they hear without a preacher?

And how shall they preach, except they be sent? As it is written, how beautiful are the feet of them that preach the gospel of peace, and bring glad tidings of good things

Romans 10:13-15

7.  **The famous blessing spoken over the Philippian church is testimony to the effect of tithes and offerings.**

The Philippian church sustained Paul on the mission field and yielded great blessings. Paul is a great example of someone who was supported by the tithes and offerings of the church. It was in response to the support that he received that he spoke the famous apostolic blessing, "But my God shall supply all your need according to his riches in glory by Christ Jesus."

You yourselves also know, Philippians, that at the first preaching of the Gospel, after I left Macedonia, no church shared with me in the matter of giving and receiving but you alone; for even in Thessalonica you sent a gift more than once for my needs.

Not that I seek the gift itself, but I seek for the profit which increases to your account.

But I have received everything in full and have an abundance; I am amply supplied, having received from Epaphroditus what you have sent, a fragrant aroma, an acceptable sacrifice, well-pleasing to God.

And my God will supply all your needs according to His riches in glory in Christ Jesus.

Philippians 4:15-19 (NASB)

*Chapter 18*

# How Tithers Invoke the Blessings of Almsgiving

ithes are also used to support the poor and unfortunate in our society. Tithers therefore always invoke the blessings of those who help the poor. When you pay your tithes, you may not have intended to help the poor but you will indirectly contribute to their lives. Tithes contribute to the upkeep of widows, orphans, aliens, and poor people. You can therefore expect many blessings to come your way because you are involved in their support.

Everyone who pays tithes has supported the poor and can expect the blessings of those who support the poor to come upon them.

1.   **Tithing fulfils God's instruction to support the poor and therefore tithers can expect the blessings of those who obey His Word.**

Also you shall not neglect the Levite who is in your town, for he has no portion or inheritance among you.

At the end of every third year you shall bring out all the tithe of your produce in that year, and shall deposit it in your town.

The Levite, because he has no portion or inheritance among you, and the alien, the orphan and the widow who are in your town, shall come and eat and be satisfied, in order that the Lord your God may bless you in all the work of your hand which you do.

Deuteronomy 14:27-29 (NASB)

**2.    Tithing fulfils God's instruction to support the poor and therefore tithers can expect to never be in need.**

HE WHO GIVES TO THE POOR WILL NEVER WANT, but he who shuts his eyes will have many curses.

Proverbs 28:27 (NASB)

**3.    Tithing fulfils God's instruction to support the poor and therefore tithers can expect to be considered as righteous.**

BECAUSE I DELIVERED THE POOR that cried, and the fatherless, and him that had none to help him.

The blessing of him that was ready to perish came upon me: and I caused the widow's heart to sing for joy.

I PUT ON RIGHTEOUSNESS, and it clothed me: my judgment was as a robe and a diadem.

I was eyes to the blind, and feet was I to the lame. I was a father to the poor: and the cause which I knew not I searched out.

Job 29:12-16

4.   **Tithing fulfils God's instruction to support the poor and therefore tithers can expect to stand guiltless before God.**

If I have withheld the poor from their desire, or have caused the eyes of the widow to fail; or have eaten my morsel myself alone, and the fatherless hath not eaten thereof;

(For from my youth he was brought up with me, as with a father, and I have guided her from my mother's womb;)

If I have seen any perish for want of clothing, or any poor without covering;

If his loins have not blessed me, and if he were not warmed with the fleece of my sheep; if I have lifted up my hand against the fatherless, when I saw my help in the gate:

THEN LET MINE ARM FALL FROM MY SHOULDER BLADE, AND MINE ARM BE BROKEN FROM THE BONE.

For destruction from God was a terror to me, and by reason of his highness I could not endure.

If I have made gold my hope, or have said to the fine gold, Thou art my confidence; if I rejoiced because my wealth was great, and because mine hand had gotten much;

If I beheld the sun when it shined, or the moon walking in brightness;

And my heart hath been secretly enticed, or my mouth hath kissed my hand:

THIS ALSO WERE AN INIQUITY TO BE PUNISHED BY THE JUDGE: FOR I SHOULD HAVE DENIED THE GOD THAT IS ABOVE.

                                                    Job 31:16-28

**5.** **Tithing fulfils God's instruction to support the poor and therefore tithers can expect to be preserved.**

BLESSED IS HE THAT CONSIDERETH THE POOR: the Lord will deliver him in time of trouble.

THE LORD WILL PRESERVE HIM, and keep him alive; and he shall be blessed upon the earth: and thou wilt not deliver him unto the will of his enemies.

The Lord will strengthen him upon the bed of languishing: thou wilt make all his bed in his sickness.

Psalm 41:1-3

**6.** **Tithing fulfils God's instruction to support the poor and therefore tithers can expect to be kept alive on the earth.**

BLESSED IS HE THAT CONSIDERETH THE POOR: the Lord will deliver him in time of trouble.

The Lord will preserve him, and KEEP HIM ALIVE; and he shall be blessed upon the earth: and thou wilt not deliver him unto the will of his enemies.

The Lord will strengthen him upon the bed of languishing: thou wilt make all his bed in his sickness.

Psalm 41:1-3

**7.** **Tithing fulfils God's instruction to support the poor and therefore tithers can expect to be blessed on the earth.**

BLESSED IS HE THAT CONSIDERETH THE POOR: the Lord will deliver him in time of trouble.

The Lord will preserve him, and keep him alive; and HE

SHALL BE BLESSED UPON THE EARTH: and thou wilt not deliver him unto the will of his enemies.

The Lord will strengthen him upon the bed of languishing: thou wilt make all his bed in his sickness.

Psalm 41:1-3

**8.  Tithing fulfils God's instruction to support the poor and therefore tithers can expect to be kept from falling into the will of the enemy.**

BLESSED IS HE THAT CONSIDERETH THE POOR: the Lord will deliver him in time of trouble.

The Lord will preserve him, and keep him alive; and he shall be blessed upon the earth: and THOU WILT NOT DELIVER HIM UNTO THE WILL OF HIS ENEMIES.

The Lord will strengthen him upon the bed of languishing: thou wilt make all his bed in his sickness.

Psalm 41:1-3

**9.  Tithing fulfils God's instruction to support the poor and therefore tithers can expect to be strengthened by God in time of difficulty.**

BLESSED IS HE THAT CONSIDERETH THE POOR: the Lord will deliver him in time of trouble.

The Lord will preserve him, and keep him alive; and he shall be blessed upon the earth: and thou wilt not deliver him unto the will of his enemies.

THE LORD WILL STRENGTHEN HIM UPON THE BED OF LANGUISHING: thou wilt make all his bed in his sickness.

Psalm 41:1-3

**10.** **Tithing fulfils God's instruction to support the poor and therefore tithers can expect God to take care of them in time of sickness.**

BLESSED IS HE THAT CONSIDERETH THE POOR: the Lord will deliver him in time of trouble.

The Lord will preserve him, and keep him alive; and he shall be blessed upon the earth: and thou wilt not deliver him unto the will of his enemies.

The Lord will strengthen him upon the bed of languishing: THOU WILT MAKE ALL HIS BED IN HIS SICKNESS.

Psalm 41:1-3

**11.** **Tithing fulfils God's instruction to support the poor and therefore tithers can expect God to pay back all the tithe they have ever given.**

He that hath pity upon the poor lendeth unto the Lord; and that which he hath given will he pay him again.

Proverbs 19:17

*Chapter 19*

# How Tithers Open the Heavens over Their Lives

1.    **Tithers cause the heavens to be opened over their lives.**

Bring ye all the tithes into the storehouse, that there may be meat in mine house, and prove me now herewith, saith the Lord of hosts, if I WILL NOT OPEN YOU THE WINDOWS OF HEAVEN, and pour you out a blessing, that there shall not be room enough to receive it.

Malachi 3:10

There is a Heaven above.  Heaven has windows.  The windows in Heaven can be opened over your life or they can be closed.  Whenever the windows of Heaven are opened, certain things take place.  The Bible is full of examples of what happens when the windows of Heaven are opened.  This chapter will help you understand exactly what happens when the windows of Heaven are opened.  Tithing is one of the ways to open the windows of Heaven over your life.  Every tither lives under "open heavens." The opening of the heavens are linked to several other significant blessings like the rebuking of devourers and destroyers. It is these different "blessings of the open heavens" that make tithing a powerful door opener for Christians.

## 2. Tithers cause the heavens to be opened over their lives and the "open heavens" means that blessings are poured out on them.

Bring ye all the tithes into the storehouse, that there may be meat in mine house, and prove me now herewith, saith the Lord of hosts, if i will not open you the windows of heaven, and POUR YOU OUT A BLESSING, that there shall not be room enough to receive it.

Malachi 3:10

The Scripture about the heavens being opened is usually interpreted to mean that the windows of Heaven will be opened and money poured out from above. But the Bible does not talk about money being poured down from the skies above. Money pouring into your house from the clouds above is a fantasy we all have. Unfortunately, money will not be poured out of Heaven per se. What will be poured out from above is called *a blessing.*

It is this blessing that we must seek and expect. There are many things that money cannot buy. Money is one of the smallest and most insignificant blessings you could ever have. I know you may find it difficult to believe that money is not such a great blessing after all. But read on and you will understand better.

In this chapter, I want you to understand what it really means for a blessing to be poured out on you from an open heaven.

The things I speak of are not my ideas and I do not pretend to have ever seen Heaven nor its windows. These things are described in the Word of God.

145

## 3.    Tithers cause the heavens to be opened over their lives and the devourer in their lives is paralyzed.

And I WILL REBUKE THE DEVOURER FOR YOUR SAKES, and he shall not destroy the fruits of your ground; neither shall your vine cast her fruit before the time in the field, saith the Lord of hosts.

Malachi 3:11

Perhaps the greatest blessing of the tithe is to have the devourer rebuked.

The creation of wealth is not dependent on how much you earn but on how much goes out of your hand.  Many people earn a lot but pay out a lot more.  This is why people with high salaries often do not have money to spend.  The devourer takes away everything.  Well-known and "established devourers" include things like the rent, the mortgage, the car bills, the water bills, the heating bills, the electricity bills, the gas bills, the property rates, poll tax, income tax, gift tax, waste management bills, staff salaries, health bills, insurance bills, shopping bills, groceries bills, parking bills, traffic over-speeding fines, etc., until there is nothing left.

Few people realise the correlation between the devourer and the creation of real wealth. People are more prosperous when they live in places with fewer devourers.  Unfortunately, places with fewer devourers are often unattractive to live in but those who have had the boldness to live in places like that usually enjoy a much higher quality of life.  Africa and other poorer developing countries have fewer "established devourers."

Years ago, my father owned a hotel and hired a manager to run it.  It was not doing very well and the income was about fifteen units of the currency.   One day, something happened and he sacked most of the staff including the manager. He then asked me if I knew anyone who could run a hotel. I said I did not know any hotel manager but I had a close friend who was honest.  He

146

asked me to bring this friend along and he hired him instantly. This friend of mine had no idea about managing a hotel but he was an honest person.

Can you believe that the income of the hotel jumped from fifteen units to about a thousand units overnight? My friend had not introduced any new hotel management ideas into the business. He just did not steal as the last group had been doing.

Suddenly, with the devourer rebuked, the income of this hotel skyrocketed. To me, that was one of the greatest lessons on the importance of rebuking the devourer. It is not about how much is coming in. It is all about how well you can paralyse the devourers around you.

Indeed, the first blessing of the tithe is to have the devourer rebuked.

Years ago, I walked through some shops in Europe with a friend of mine who was, unknown to me, a petty thief. To my utter surprise, when we came out of the shop she showed me the things she had stolen. I could not believe my eyes but she was excited about her booty.

She told me that it was something she did all the time. Then I realised that there were many people like that who constantly stole from large shops and supermarkets. It is no wonder that many people who have large shops and supermarkets rarely make profits. The devourers walk through the shops and take away all the profit.

After this event, I noticed a trend in which shops began to invest in CCTV and other modern forms of security. Through various innovative and hi-tech measures, many large shops and supermarkets have fought the stealing menace and become profitable again.

Indeed, the profitability of these shops simply depended on fighting the devourer. This is the very thing that God promises to do when you pay your tithes. Tithe paying invokes the significant blessing of having the devourer rebuked.

Once the devourer is rebuked in your life, your wealth and assets will begin to increase. This is why people who pay tithes can become rich – the devourers in their lives are rebuked by the Lord.

## 4. Tithers cause the heavens to be opened over their lives and the destroyer is restrained.

And I will rebuke the devourer for your sakes, and HE SHALL NOT DESTROY THE FRUITS OF YOUR GROUND; neither shall your vine cast her fruit before the time in the field, saith the LORD of hosts.

Malachi 3:11

The next blessing of the tithe is to have the destroyer rebuked. The creation of wealth is linked to the prevention of destructive forces in your life. Countries that are impoverished are countries where the destroyer has had a free hand for many years.

One day, a brother built a hospital and worked very hard to build a gynaecology unit. He kept investing and working as hard as he could. He would be at the hospital day and night, caring for the different patients that came to him. One day, he asked his nurse to wheel the scanner to the bedside of a patient. This nurse pushed the delicate and expensive machine carelessly and it fell over. The new and expensive equipment this doctor had acquired had suddenly been destroyed along with thousands of dollars of hard-earned money. In one moment the hard-earned income of this doctor went down the drain.

Dear friend, this is what God promises to protect you from. In one hour, all your work and profit can come to nothing. The blessing of the tithe is the blessing of having the destroyer rebuked.

I remember the testimony of a brother who refused to pay his tithes. He was a taxi driver in a large European city. He told me how he would go out working on Sundays because he felt he needed to have money and could not afford to sacrifice his Sundays for church.

One Sunday, whilst working he scratched somebody's car slightly. He searched in vain to find the owner of the car. Finally, when he could not find the driver, he left a note on the person's car with his number. He did not hear from anyone until the police caught up with him and charged him with a "hit and run" charge. He was astonished and protested to the police, "It was not a hit and run case. I left my number. Unfortunately and unknown to this brother, one of the digits of his number was unclear and they were unable to call him.

In the end, he was forced to fix the car of the person whose car he had scratched plus his own car and also pay fines to the police for a hit and run offence.

He lamented about how he had spent thousands of dollars of hard-earned money to sort this case out. Then he confessed that if he had been in church and paid tithes he would have been far better of. The destroyer had had free access to his life and eaten away a whole year's income.

God promises to rebuke the destroyer when you pay your tithes. Destruction will not eat away all you have laboured for. God will bless you because you pay your tithes and destroyers will have no power over you.

## 5. Tithers cause the heavens to be opened over their lives and the "open heavens" means that you will be called blessed by all nations.

And ALL NATIONS SHALL CALL YOU BLESSED: for ye shall be a delightsome land, saith the LORD of hosts.

Malachi 3:12

When you pay your tithes, the blessing of the Lord will descend on you and everyone will notice that you are blessed. Your blessings will become more and more evident because that is one of the blessings of the tithe. Do you want to be blessed in such a way that everyone will see that you are blessed? Begin tithing and pay your tithes for years. It will surely happen in your life.

## 6. Tithers cause the heavens to be opened over their lives and the "open heavens" means that you will be called a delightsome land.

Paying of tithes causes a blessing to be poured out on you and one of the effects of that blessing is that you will be called a delightsome land. You will be attractive and bring pleasure to people.

And all nations shall call you blessed: FOR YE SHALL BE A DELIGHTSOME LAND, saith the Lord of hosts.

Malachi 3:12

## 7. Tithers cause the heavens to be opened over their lives and the "open heavens" means that you will be blessed to see visions of God.

Now it came to pass in the thirtieth year, in the fourth month, in the fifth day of the month, as I was among the captives by the river of Chebar, that THE HEAVENS WERE OPENED, AND I SAW VISIONS of God.

Ezekiel 1:1

When the heavens were opened, Ezekiel saw visions of God.

But how is the paying of tithes connected to the seeing of visions? Most people do not connect the paying of tithes with the seeing of visions. But paying of tithes causes the heavens to be opened and the opening of the heavens causes you to see visions of God.

Visions can change your life permanently. One of the little known blessings of tithing is to see visions. My life has been blessed greatly by the visions God has given me and I recommend that you pay your tithes so that the heavens will be opened and you will have visions of God.

**8.  Tithers cause the heavens to be opened over their lives and the "open heavens" means that the Holy Spirit will be openly manifest in your life.**

Then cometh Jesus from Galilee to Jordan unto John, to be baptized of him.

But John forbad him, saying, I have need to be baptized of thee, and comest thou to me?

And Jesus answering said unto him, Suffer it to be so now: for thus it becometh us to fulfil all righteousness. Then he suffered him.

And Jesus, when he was baptized, went up straightway out of the water: and, lo, THE HEAVENS WERE OPENED unto him, and HE SAW THE SPIRIT OF GOD DESCENDING like a dove, and lighting upon him:

And lo a voice from heaven, saying, This is my beloved Son, in whom I am well pleased.

Matthew 3:13-17

When there is an open heaven the Holy Spirit is poured out on you.  When you pay your tithes the Holy Spirit will be poured upon you because of the open heavens. You will have the spirit of wisdom, knowledge, understanding, might and counsel.  You will have the helper in your life.

All the blessings of the coming of the anointing will be your portion because of the open heavens over your life.

**9.  Tithers cause the heavens to be opened over their lives and the "open heavens" means that you will see the glory of God in your life.**

But he, being full of the Holy Ghost, looked up stedfastly into heaven, and SAW THE GLORY OF GOD, and Jesus standing on the right hand of God, and said, Behold, I SEE THE

HEAVENS OPENED, and the Son of man standing on the right hand of God.

Acts 7:55-56

The tithe opens the windows of Heaven and when the windows of Heaven are opened the glory of God pours out on your life.

The glory of God speaks of the beauty of the Lord. If God beautifies you and all that you are, you will be truly beautiful. The glory of God is different from the glory of man. Man is attracted to the outward appearance but God has things that attract Him. A meek, humble and quiet spirit is precious to the Lord. When the glory of the Lord is upon you, a serene heavenly beauty will descend on your life. You will be glorious in the sight of the Lord. What a blessing an open Heaven brings into your life!

## 10. Tithers cause the heavens to be open over their lives and the "open heavens" means that you will see Jesus.

But he, being full of the Holy Ghost, looked up stedfastly into heaven, and saw the glory of God, and Jesus standing on the right hand of God, and said, Behold, I SEE THE HEAVENS OPENED, AND THE SON OF MAN STANDING on the right hand of God.

Acts 7:55-56

When the windows of Heaven opened, Stephen saw Jesus standing by the right hand of God. But what is the connection between Jesus appearing to you and the paying of your tithes? Is the paying of your tithes a gate fee that gives you access to Jesus? No, the tithe is not a gate fee but it has the effect of opening the windows of Heaven over your life. When the windows of Heaven are opened over your life, you can expect to see Jesus just as Stephen did.

One of greatest blessings you could ever have is for Jesus to appear to you. I have prayed for years that I might see Jesus. Years ago, I read about how Kenneth Hagin saw the Lord. His descriptions of those encounters enthralled me. I read them over and over again, gleaning what I could for myself.

Since then, I have had a longing to see Jesus. I want Him to appear to me and speak to me. I want Him to tell me whether I am doing the right thing or not. But such a blessing is not easily acquired. It takes the heavens being opened. I feel so encouraged to find out that paying tithes can open the heavens over my life. I feel so blessed to be able to pay my tithes. I want to pay more tithes! I want to open the windows of Heaven over my life. I want to see Jesus.

*Chapter 20*

# Ten Things That Happen Every Time You Tithe

## 1. Every time you tithe, YOU HONOUR GOD.

Every time you tithe, you show respect to God. God receives the honour of you giving the first part of your income to Him. This is the greatest act of respect you can show to the Lord.

Honour the Lord with thy substance, and with the firstfruits of all thine increase: so shall thy barns be filled with plenty, and thy presses shall burst out with new wine.

Proverbs 3:9-10

## 2. Every time you tithe, YOU REMEMBER GOD. Tithing demonstrates that you remember God. There is a very strong exhortation to remember the Lord in all things. It is easy to forget the invisible hand of the Lord that has made everything possible.

BEWARE THAT THOU FORGET NOT THE LORD THY GOD, in not keeping his commandments, and his judgments, and his statutes, which I command thee this day: Lest when thou hast eaten and art full, and hast built goodly houses, and dwelt therein; And when thy herds and thy flocks multiply, and thy silver and thy gold is multiplied, and all that thou hast is multiplied; Then thine heart be lifted up, and THOU FORGET THE LORD THY GOD, which brought thee forth out of the land of Egypt, from the house of bondage; Who led thee through that great and terrible wilderness, wherein were fiery serpents, and scorpions, and drought, where there was no water; who brought thee forth water out of the rock of flint; Who fed thee in the wilderness with manna, which thy fathers knew not, that he might humble thee, and that he might prove thee, to do thee good at thy latter end; And thou say in thine heart, My power and the might of mine hand hath gotten me this wealth. BUT THOU SHALT REMEMBER THE LORD THY GOD: FOR IT IS HE THAT GIVETH THEE POWER TO GET WEALTH, that he may establish his covenant which he sware unto thy fathers, as it is this day. And it shall be, if thou do at all forget the Lord thy God, and walk after other gods, and serve them, and worship them, I testify against you this day that ye shall surely perish. As the nations which the Lord destroyeth before your face, so shall ye perish; because ye would not be obedient unto the voice of the Lord your God.

Deuteronomy 8:11-20

3. **Every time you tithe, YOU WORSHIP GOD.** Traditionally, worship is seen as singing a few slow songs in church. The fast songs are seen as praises and the slow songs are deemed to be worship. But the Scripture reveals that worship is much more than that. Tithing is *also* an act of worship. Coming to the house of God and presenting Him with your tithes is a wonderful act of worship.

And now, behold, I have brought the firstfruits of the land, which thou, O Lord, hast given me. And thou shalt set it before the Lord thy God, and WORSHIP before the Lord thy God:

Deuteronomy 26:10

155

**4. Every time you tithe, YOU SHOW YOUR RESPECT FOR HOLY THINGS.** Every time you tithe, you show your regard for things that God has declared sacred. Every time you tithe, you show that you know the difference between what God has called special and what is ordinary. Showing respect for holy things is the same as showing respect for God's things.

And concerning the tithe of the herd, or of the flock, even of whatsoever passeth under the rod, THE TENTH SHALL BE HOLY UNTO THE LORD. He shall not search whether it be good or bad, neither shall he change it: and if he change it at all, then both it and the change thereof shall be holy; it shall not be redeemed.

Leviticus 27:32-33

Then thou shalt say before the Lord thy God, I HAVE BROUGHT AWAY THE HALLOWED THINGS OUT OF MINE HOUSE, AND ALSO HAVE GIVEN THEM UNTO THE LEVITE, and unto the stranger, to the fatherless, and to the widow, ACCORDING TO ALL THY COMMANDMENTS WHICH THOU HAST COMMANDED ME: I have not transgressed thy commandments, neither have I forgotten them:

Deuteronomy 26:13

**5. Every time you tithe, YOU OBEY GOD.** Obedience to the commandments of the Lord is demonstrated every time you pay your tithes. In the natural, tithing does not make sense. If you need more money, what could be more foolish than throwing away some of your money? But every time you pay your tithes you demonstrate obedience to the Most High God. You will never lose your blessing for this. All the blessed people of the Bible received their blessing in exactly the same way – through obedience.

I have not eaten thereof in my mourning, neither have I taken away ought thereof for any unclean use, nor given ought

156

thereof for the dead: but I have hearkened to the voice of the Lord my God, and have done according to all that thou hast commanded me.

Deuteronomy 26:14

6. **Every time you tithe, YOU DEMONSTRATE FAITH IN GOD.** Faith is seeing the invisible. Every time you tithe, you demonstrate that you believe in the existence of the invisible powers of God. If you see it, it is not faith. Faith is the substance of things you do not see. We cannot see the effect of our giving but we believe that it works a mighty work on our behalf in the spirit realm.

Bring ye all the tithes into the storehouse, that there may be meat in mine house, and PROVE ME now herewith, saith the Lord of hosts, if I will not open you the windows of heaven, and pour you out a blessing, that there shall not be room enough to receive it.

Malachi 3:10-11

7. **Every time you tithe, YOU APPRECIATE FULL-TIME MINISTRY.** Tithes were primarily used to support the Levites. The Levites represent the apostles, prophets, pastors and evangelists of today. Without a deep understanding of the importance of ministry, you would not fork out a percentage of your income for the support of this "club." Unspiritual people do not consider it necessary to support apostles, prophets, teachers and pastors. However, as the years go by, you will discover the importance of these men of God. You will grow in your desire to do anything to support them. Indeed, your ability to persistently pay your tithes demonstrates your deep understanding of God's gifts to you.

And I perceived that the portions of the Levites had not been given them: for the Levites and the singers, that did the work, were fled every one to his field.

Nehemiah 13:10

157

8. **Every time you tithe, YOU DEMONSTRATE YOUR BELIEF IN ETERNITY.** Every time you tithe, you demonstrate that you have another world in view. The Scripture teaches us to lay up treasures in heaven. The way to lay up treasures in Heaven is to invest in the kingdom of God. Paying tithes is a powerful demonstration of your understanding of eternal judgement.

When you have eternal values you are conscious of the fact that you will be judged for every dollar you steal from God. Because of your fear of God and your consciousness of eternity tithing will be easy for you. Every time you tithe, you demonstrate your belief in the reality of eternity.

Lay not up for yourselves treasures upon earth, where moth and rust doth corrupt, and where thieves break through and steal: but lay up for yourselves treasures in heaven, where neither moth nor rust doth corrupt, and where thieves do not break through nor steal:

*Matthew 6:19-20*

9. **Every time you tithe, YOU OBTAIN A BLESSING AND AVOID A CURSE.** A person who tithes, opens the door for blessings in his life. The curse of the devourer and the destroyer are broken. He enters into a blessing and walks away from many evils.

Will a man rob God? Yet ye have robbed me. But ye say, Wherein have we robbed thee? In tithes and offerings. Ye are cursed with a curse: for ye have robbed me, even this whole nation.

*Malachi 3:8-9*

10. **Every time you tithe, YOU DEMONSTRATE YOUR KNOWLEDGE OF THE SOURCE OF YOUR BLESSINGS.** Everything we have comes from God. The fool says in his heart, "There is no God." Fools say they have acquired all they have through their own strength and

through their own hand. Hosea had occasion to rebuke the people of Israel because they did not realise where their blessings came from. "For she did not know that I gave her corn, and wine, and oil, and multiplied her silver and gold, which they prepared for Baal. Therefore will I return, and take away my corn in the time thereof, and my wine in the season thereof, and will recover my wool and my flax given to cover her nakedness" (Hosea 2:8-9).

Throughout the ages, spiritual men and women who feared God declared, "all that I am and all that I have comes from thee." Listen to the words of King David:

Wherefore David blessed the LORD before all the congregation: and David said, Blessed be thou, LORD God of Israel our father, for ever and ever.

Thine, O LORD, is the greatness, and the power, and the glory, and the victory, and the majesty: for all that is in the heaven and in the earth is thine; thine is the kingdom, O LORD, and thou art exalted as head above all.

Both riches and honour come of thee, and thou reignest over all; and in thine hand is power and might; and in thine hand it is to make great, and to give strength unto all.

Now therefore, our God, we thank thee, and praise thy glorious name.

But who am I, and what is my people, that we should be able to offer so willingly after this sort? for all things come of thee, and of thine own have we given thee.

1 Chronicles 29:10-14

*Chapter 21*

# Why Tithing is the First Step into Ministry

Tithing, unlike other freewill offerings, demands ten percent of your life. It is therefore the first real contribution that you make towards the work of God. Most other offerings you make are an insignificant fraction of your income. The tithe takes away ten percent of everything you have done and earned for yourself. This is why tithing is the first serious step towards the things of God.

Tithing therefore puts you in real contact with the work of the ministry. Ten percent of your life is committed to help the things of God. Indeed, there is no greater blessing than the blessing of being called to work for the Lord. No amount of money could ever compare with the privilege of working in the ministry.

Tithing takes you much further than mere financial harvests. It takes you into the realm of the high calling to ministry. This is the job that very few human beings will ever have the opportunity to do.

1. **Tithing is your first step to the obedience of minor instructions that will prepare you for weightier matters of ministry.** Jesus described judgment, mercy and faith as "weightier matters." This implied that tithing was not as important as mercy, judgement and faith. Tithing is a minor instruction as compared to mercy, judgement and faith. If you are not faithful with the minor issues, how can you be trusted with "weightier matters"? When you pay your tithes you pass the test of demonstrating faithfulness with minor matters. You also demonstrate that you are ready to take up the weightier matters of ministry.

   Woe unto you, scribes and Pharisees, hypocrites! for ye pay tithe of mint and anise and cummin, AND HAVE OMITTED THE WEIGHTIER MATTERS OF THE LAW, judgment, mercy, and faith: these ought ye to have done, and not to leave the other undone.

   Matthew 23:23

2. **Paying your tithes is your first step towards understanding God's pattern for ministry.** God's pattern for ministry is that the Levites should be supported through the tithes of the people whilst they busy themselves with God's work. This is the pattern that was set by Moses and it is the pattern which is used by the New Testament church.

   Thou shalt truly tithe all the increase of thy seed, that the field bringeth forth year by year. And thou shalt eat before the LORD thy God, in the place which he shall choose to place his name there, the tithe of thy corn, of thy wine, and of thine oil, and the firstlings of thy herds and of thy flocks; THAT THOU MAYEST LEARN to fear the Lord they God always.

   Deuteronomy 14:22-23

3. **Paying your tithes is your first step towards respecting the ministry.** Paying tithes is your first chance to show respect for the things of God. It is your first chance to show respect for ministers and their calling. Many Christians do not

respect the ministry; that is why they do not want their children to be priests or pastors. I have watched how Christian families send their favourite children to universities to become doctors and lawyers but send their mentally-retarded children to the Bible school. These are all signs of disrespect. In their sub-conscious mind they think that some people are too intelligent to become priests.

Thou shalt truly tithe all the increase of thy seed, that the field bringeth forth year by year. And thou shalt eat before the Lord thy God, in the place which he shall choose to place his name there, the tithe of thy corn, of thy wine, and of thine oil, and the firstlings of thy herds and of thy flocks; THAT THOU MAYEST LEARN TO FEAR THE LORD THY GOD ALWAYS.

Deuteronomy 14:22-23

4. **Paying your tithes is your first step towards understanding the inner workings of ministry.** How do churches survive? How are pastors paid? How do pastors' families survive? The tithe is the answer to all these questions. Every time you pay your tithes, you demonstrate an understanding of these intimate aspects of ministry.

For it is written in the law of Moses, Thou shalt not muzzle the mouth of the ox that treadeth out the corn. Doth God take care for oxen?

1 Corinthians 9:9

5. **Paying your tithes is your first step towards a real contribution to ministry.** Perhaps one day you will work full-time for the Lord. But until then, your tithe is your first real contribution to the ministry. Your tithe respresents ten percent of your time, effort, work and money. It is a very substantial contribution to God's work.

And I perceived that the portions of the Levites had not been given them: for the Levites and the singers, that did the work, were fled every one to his field. Then contended I with the rulers, and said, Why is the house of God forsaken? And I gathered them together, and set them in their place. Then brought all Judah the tithe of the corn and the new wine and the oil unto the treasuries.

Nehemiah 13:10-12

6. **Paying your tithes is your first step towards appreciating the work of a priest.**

AND THIS SHALL BE THE PRIEST'S DUE FROM THE PEOPLE, from them that offer a sacrifice, whether it be ox or sheep; and they shall give unto the priest the shoulder, and the two cheeks, and the maw. THE FIRSTFRUIT also of thy corn, of thy wine, and of thine oil, and the first of the fleece of thy sheep, shalt thou give him. For the LORD thy God hath chosen him out of all thy tribes, to stand to minister in the name of the Lord, him and his sons for ever.

Deuteronomy 18:3-5

7. **Paying your tithes is the first step towards a covenant.** God had a covenant with Aaron in which Aaron became a priest forever. The covenant stated that Aaron's descendants would be priests who would have no inheritance but the Lord.

Every time you pay tithes, you demonstrate your understanding of God's covenant with the priesthood. This prepares you for your own covenant of ministry with God.

And thou shalt anoint Aaron and his sons, and consecrate them, that they may minister unto me in the priest's office.

And thou shalt speak unto the children of Israel, saying, This shall be an holy anointing oil unto me throughout your generations.

Exodus 30:30-31

All the offerings of the holy gifts, which the sons of Israel offer to the Lord , I have given to you and your sons and your daughters with you, as a perpetual allotment. It is an everlasting covenant of salt before the Lord to you and your descendants with you."

Then the Lord said to Aaron, "You shall have no inheritance in their land nor own any portion among them; I am your portion and your inheritance among the sons of Israel.

Numbers 18:19-20 (NASB)

*Chapter 22*

# Ten Reasons Why Tithing Does Not Work for Some People

**… all things work together …**

**Romans 8:28**

M any things work together to create the blessings we need. Success is often the result of several things working together.

Tithing cannot be studied in isolation. Obeying God in the matter of tithing is just one of many commandments of the Lord. It is good that you would obey the Lord in paying your tithes but you must also obey the Lord in other areas.

When the apostle Peter spoke of bearing fruit and being useful to God, he mentioned several things that would have to work together to make you fruitful. "Now for this very reason also, applying all diligence, in your faith supply moral excellence, and in your moral excellence, knowledge, and in your knowledge, self-control, and in your self-control, perseverance, and in your perseverance, godliness, and in your godliness, brotherly kindness, and in your brotherly kindness, love. For if these qualities are yours and are increasing, they render you neither useless nor unfruitful in the true knowledge of our Lord Jesus Christ" (2 Peter 1:5-8, NASB).

You can see from this Scripture that it takes many things to make a person fruitful.

In this chapter, I will share with you things that need to work together with tithing in order to produce the blessing.

## Ten Reasons Why Tithing Does Not Work for Some People

**1. Tithing does not work for some people because they do not recognize God's provision when it comes.**

God's way of rewarding you for tithing may not be what you expect. There are many things which are "priceless". Their value exceeds any amount of dollars you could put together.

God often gives His children things, which are beyond price only for them to turn around and say He has not blessed them.

Naaman, the Syrian, expected Elisha to heal him in a particular way. He almost missed his blessing because he expected God to work in a particular way. It was a little child who gave him much needed advice.

"My father, if the prophet had bid thee do some great thing, wouldest thou not have done it? how much rather then, when he saith to thee, Wash, and be clean? Then went he down, and dipped himself seven times in Jordan, according to the saying of the man of God: and his flesh came again like unto the flesh of a little child, and he was clean" (2 Kings 5:13-14 ).

Do not become ungrateful because God's blessing has come to you in a slightly different way from what you expected.

## 2. Tithing does not work for some people because it is not the first thing they give.

Also that day they offered great sacrifices, and rejoiced: for God had made them rejoice with great joy: the wives also and the children rejoiced: so that the joy of Jerusalem was heard even afar off.

And at that time were some appointed over the chambers for the treasures, for the offerings, for THE FIRSTFRUITS, and for THE TITHES, to gather into them out of the fields of the cities the portions of the law for the priests and Levites: for Judah rejoiced for the priests and for the Levites that waited.

Nehemiah 12:43-44

THE TITHE IS THE *FIRST* FRUITS OF YOUR INCREASE. IT IS NOT THE *LAST* FRUITS OF YOUR SURPLUS. The tithe is a ministration of respect and honour to God. Perhaps the greatest show of respect and honour to God is in the fact that it is the first thing you do with your money. The tithe changes in its very nature when it is not done first. This may be the reason why somebody may give ten percent of his money but not see the increase. Years ago, when we began our church, we called our tithes the "first and best fruits." Giving the first and the best of what you have is foundational to proper tithing.

## 3. Tithing does not work for some people because it is not ten percent of their income.

The tithe simply means ten percent. Nine percent is not a tithe! Eight percent is not a tithe! Seven percent is not a tithe! Six percent is not a tithe! Five percent is not a tithe! Four percent is not a tithe! Three percent is not a tithe! Two percent is not a tithe! One percent is not a tithe! THE TITHE IS TEN PERCENT.

I believe that even someone in class three would know how to calculate ten percent. Do you think that God and His angels are able to calculate ten percent? Begin to give at least ten percent of your increase and God's blessing will come upon your life. The tithe is ten percent of your increase. That is what God honours.

### 4.   Tithing does not work for some people because it is not an acceptable offering.

The fact that your money entered the offering bowl does not mean that it was accepted in Heaven. Some tithes are also unacceptable because the tithe is a special type of offering.

There are three types of offerings that are unacceptable to God. Offerings are unacceptable to God because of the unrighteous lives of the giver, the secret worship of idols and thirdly not having given in proportion to what we received. Notice these three times the Lord warns us about unacceptable offerings.

a.   In the book of Isaiah, the Lord rejects the offerings of the people because of their unrighteous lives. Read it for yourself. He tells them, "Learn to do well. Relieve the oppressed. Help the fatherless and widows."

**To what purpose is the multitude of your sacrifices unto me? saith the LORD: I am full of the burnt offerings of rams, and the fat of fed beasts; and I delight not in the blood of bullocks, or of lambs, or of he goats.**

**When ye come to appear before me, who hath required this at your hand, to tread my courts?**

**Bring no more vain oblations; incense is an abomination unto me; the new moons and sabbaths, the calling of assemblies, I CANNOT AWAY WITH; IT IS INIQUITY, even the solemn meeting.**

**Your new moons and your appointed feasts my soul hateth: they are a trouble unto me; I am weary to bear them.**

And when ye spread forth your hands, I will hide mine eyes from you: yea, when ye make many prayers, I will not hear: your hands are full of blood.

Wash you, make you clean; put away the evil of your doings from before mine eyes; cease to do evil;

Learn to do well; seek judgment, relieve the oppressed, judge the fatherless, plead for the widow.

**Isaiah 1:11-17**

b.    In the book of Amos God rejects the offerings they bring because they were secretly worshipping the gods Moloch and Chiun.

**THOUGH YE OFFER ME BURNT OFFERINGS AND YOUR MEAT OFFERINGS, I WILL NOT ACCEPT THEM:** neither will I regard the peace offerings of your fat beasts.

Take thou away from me the noise of thy songs; for I will not hear the melody of thy viols.

But let judgment run down as waters, and righteousness as a mighty stream.

Have ye offered unto me sacrifices and offerings in the wilderness forty years, O house of Israel?

But ye have borne the tabernacle of your Moloch and Chiun your images, the star of your god, which ye made to yourselves.

Therefore will I cause you to go into captivity beyond Damascus, saith the LORD, whose name is The God of hosts.

**Amos 5:22-27**

c.  In the book of Corinthians, Paul shows that offerings are accepted when they are in proportion to what a person has. God always looks at what you have before assessing what you have brought to Him. You may bring a hundred thousand dollars to the altar but because you have billions this amount may not impress the Lord.

**[Your offering] is accepted according to that a man hath, and not according to that he hath not.**

**2 Corinthians 8:12**

## 5. Tithing does not work for some people because they do not have patience.

**For ye have need of patience, that, after ye have done the will of God, ye might receive the promise.**

**Hebrews 10:36**

You need patience to be successful in every field of endeavour. Even in the secular world, patience is important. There is almost nothing you are going to get in this world without patience. It took me seven years of hard labour to become a medical doctor. I had to wait patiently and allow the years to roll by until I was finally declared a doctor. If you want to see the powerful effect of tithing, you will need patience.

Why do you think I have written about the wealth of the Jews in this book. It is a testimony to the powerful effects of tithing. Thousands of years of tithing have produced an important pattern that is difficult to ignore. Years of tithing by Jews, has produced the wealthiest ethnic group in America (of all places). What else could be a greater testimony to the powerful effect of tithing? Tithing will seem not to work for you when you do not have patience. Indeed, with patience you will discover for yourself that tithing truly works. It produces wealth. It produces blessings! Allow patience to work in your life and you will see the blessings. "For ye have need of patience, that, after ye have done the will of God, ye might receive the promise" (Hebrews 10:36).

## 6.    Tithing does not work for some people because of their negative confessions.

Tithing does not work for some people because of their negative confessions. It is important that you maintain positive confessions about your life. What is the point in paying tithes and canceling the blessings of tithing with your negative confessions?

The principles of tithing work together with the principles of faith. "For verily I say unto you, That whosoever shall say unto this mountain, Be thou removed, and be thou cast into the sea; and shall not doubt in his heart, but shall believe that those things which he saith shall come to pass; HE SHALL HAVE WHATSOEVER HE SAITH" (Mark 11:23).

## 7.    Tithing does not work for some people because they have wrong desires.

Having wrong desires contradicts other principles that are set in motion by tithing.

If you have desires to kill and to fight, God cannot bless you. In fact He may send His angels to oppose you. What is the point in paying tithes to open the windows of Heaven only to have angels fighting you from another angle? Do not forget ALL THINGS WORK TOGETHER for your good!

**Ye lust, and have not: ye kill, and desire to have, and cannot obtain: ye fight and war, yet ye have not, because ye ask not. Ye ask, and receive not, because ye ask amiss, that ye may consume it upon your lusts.**

**James 4:2-3**

## 8.    Tithing does not work for some people because they are not at peace with the brethren.

The fruit of righteousness is sown in peace by peaceful men. Strife with the brethren is not something God will bless. The

Bible teaches clearly that faith works by love. All the things you want to do for God must be done by and through Christian love. A humble loving person looks deceptively weak, but in actual fact he is strong. Love is the foundation of every spiritual thing we want to do because God is love.

**And the fruit of righteousness is sown in peace of them that make peace.**

**James 3:18**

## 9. Tithing does not work for some people because they have bad marital relationships.

Many Christians have troubled marriages. Love is often replaced with strife. Hearts once filled with love are now charged with unforgiveness and bitterness. The challenges of marriage cause many Christians to walk out of the will of God and into the domain of Satan.

A combination of strife, bitterness, unforgiveness and hatred often serve to neutralize the prayers of the saints. Blessings should fall on people who pray but because of marital conflicts many prayers are not heard. These are not my ideas. Read it for yourself: "Likewise, ye husbands, dwell with them according to knowledge, giving honour unto the wife, as unto the weaker vessel, and as being heirs together of the grace of life; that your prayers be not hindered" (1 Peter 3:7).

These problems neutralize the blessings that pours out on someone who pays his tithes.

## 10. Tithing does not work for some people because of hidden sins.

**He that covereth his sins shall not prosper: but whoso confesseth and forsaketh them shall have mercy.**

**Proverbs 28:13**

He that pays his tithes shall prosper. This is what we believe. But he that covereth his sin shall not prosper. This combination of "thou shall prosper" and "thou shall not prosper" reveal how a blessing in one area can be cancelled by a curse from another area. Many things work together. Hidden sin in our lives will fight the blessings that we invoke on ourselves by tithing.

Dear friend, to the making of many books there is no end. By these few words be admonished and be blessed! What else can I say to convince you to pay your tithes? This is a book God told me to write and I am sure the words I have shared so far will help you and your followers to find the perfect will of God. May the Lord bless you and may you find many blessings and fulfilled promises as you honour the Lord with your tithes and first fruits.

# Notes

1. Mark Twain, "Concerning the Jews," *Harper's Magazine* (September 1898).

2. Thomas Sowell, *Ethnic America* (Basic Books, 1981), 5.

3. Steven Silbiger, *The Jewish Phenomenon* (Lanham, Maryland: Rowman & Littlefield Publishing Group, 2000), 5.

4. Ibid., 8.

5. Ibid., 14-15.

6. Ibid., 42-43.

7. Ibid., 39.

8. Joshua Halberstam, *Schmoozing: The Private Conversations of American Jews* (Perigree Books, 1997), 16.

9. Alan Dershowitz, *The Vanishing American Jew* (Simon & Schuster, 1997), 16.

10. Jack Wertheimer, "Current Trends in Jewish Philanthropy," *American Jewish Yearbook*, 1997.

11. Steven Silbiger, *The Jewish Phenomenon*, 40.

12. Ibid., 40.

13. Rabbi Daniel Lapin, *Thou Shall Prosper* (Hoboken, New Jersey: John Wiley & Sons Inc., 2002), 297-298.

14. Ibid., 299-300.

15. Ibid., 302.

16. Ibid., 304, 306.

17. Ibid., 312-313.

18. Ibid., 313.

19. Naomi Mauer, "Tithing" *The Jewish Press*, September 7, 2001).

# Other Books by Dag Heward-Mills